An....... ....
Guide to
Dining, Lodging,
and Tourism

Amana Colonies Guide to Dining, Lodging, and Tourism

James Strohman

Iowa State University Press ■ Ames

© 1997 Iowa State University Press, Ames, Iowa 50014
All rights reserved

Authorization to photocopy items for internal or personal use, or the internal or personal use of specific clients, is granted by Iowa State University Press, provided that the base fee of $.10 per copy is paid directly to the Copyright Clearance Center, 27 Congress Street, Salem, MA 01970. For those organizations that have been granted a photocopy license by CCC, a separate system of payments has been arranged. The fee code for users of the Transactional Reporting Service is 0-8138-2836-8/97 $.10.

∞ Printed on acid-free paper in the United States of America

First edition, 1997

Library of Congress Cataloging-in-Publication Data

Strohman, James
Amana Colonies guide to dining, lodging, and tourism / James Strohman. — 1st ed.
    p.   cm.
Includes bibliographical references and index.
ISBN 0-8138-2836-8 (acid-free)
1. Restaurants—Iowa—Amana Region—Guidebooks.
2. Hotels—Iowa—Amana Region—Guidebooks.
3. Tourist trade—Iowa—Amana Region.
4. Amana (Iowa)—Guidebooks.   I. Title.
    TX907.3.I82A457   1997
647.95777'653—dc21   97-11967

Cover photos: (*from top*) Food served Amana family-style at the Ox Yoke Inn; mahogany frame bed from the Corner House Bed and Breakfast; communal kitchen, now the Museum of Amana History. Photos printed with permission.

The last digit is the print number: 9 8 7 6 5 4 3 2 1

To my parents

Joseph and Kathleen Strohman

of North English, Iowa,

who raised me near the Amana Colonies

and gave me

an appreciation for travel.

Contents

Acknowledgments ix

Welcome to the Amana Colonies 3
    How to Use This Guide 3
    Opportunities for Visitors 3
    Annual Events in the Amana Colonies 5
    Art and Craft Demonstrations 6
    Definition of Terms 7
    A History of the Amana Colonies 9

Amana 29
    Restaurants 33
    Lodging Facilities 50
    Shops and Tourist Attractions 56

East Amana 87

High Amana 91
    Shops and Tourist Attractions 93

Homestead 95
    Restaurants 97
    Lodging Facilities 103
    Shops and Tourist Attractions 109

Middle Amana 113
    Restaurants 115
    Lodging Facilities 119
    Shops and Tourist Attractions 126

Contents

South Amana   135
    Lodging Facilities   137
    Shops and Tourist Attractions   142

West Amana   149
    Lodging Facilities   150
    Shops and Tourist Attractions   153

Little Amana Interstate Complex and Vicinity   157
    Restaurants   160
    Lodging Facilities, Exit 225   166
    Lodging Facilities, Exit 220   169
    Lodging Facilities, Exit 216   171
    Shops and Tourist Attractions   172

Tourist Assistance Information   175

Further Reading   179

Subject Index   183

Index   189

Acknowledgments

I wish to thank the friendly and helpful residents of the Amana Colonies who assisted me or provided information. These include the proprietors and staff of the restaurants, lodging facilities, shops, and attractions listed in this guide, and the helpful and knowledgeable volunteers who work at the four museums operated by the Amana Heritage Society.

At the Museum of Amana History, particular thanks go to Barbara Hoehnle, Catherine Guerra, Erna Fels, director Lanny Haldy, and the volunteer staff.

I wish to thank my wife, Kristin Peyton, for her assistance and support and my children, Isaac Oak, Ambrose Lane, and Stella Maris, for providing constant inspiration.

For proofreading and offering suggestions, I thank Kristin Peyton and Mark Hunacek.

Special thanks to the professional staff at Iowa State University Press.

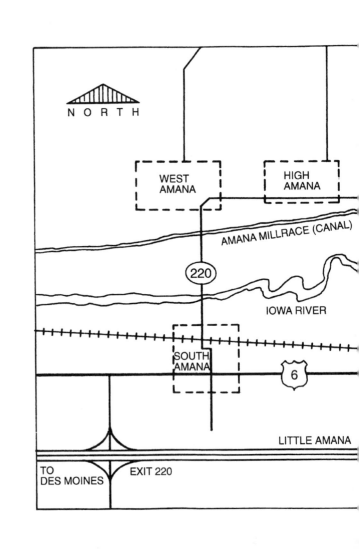

Amana Colonies Guide to Dining, Lodging, and Tourism

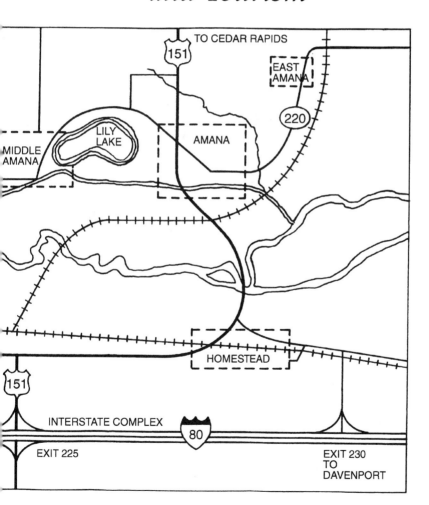

Colony residents make their way back from **Liebesmahl**, *a special religious communion ceremony. The view is the Amana main street looking east, circa 1900. (Photo courtesy Amana Heritage Society.)*

Welcome to the Amana Colonies

How to Use This Guide

This travel guide is divided by village, with a chapter on each of the seven villages of the Amana Colonies. Within the chapters are listings for village restaurants, lodging facilities, shops and tourist attractions. These listings give tourists useful information and a description of what the facility, shop, or attraction has to offer.

Three other chapters cover the Little Amana interstate complex, tourist assistance information, and further reading on the Colonies. The chapter on the Little Amana interstate complex lists the available restaurants, shops, and lodging facilities in the Little Amana area. The chapter on tourist assistance information provides locations of ATM machines, souces of fuel, automobile repair, medical care, and other useful contacts. It also lists area religious services for many denominations. The last chapter lists sources in which interested readers can find more information about the Amana Colonies.

I hope this guide will help you to get the most out of your trip to the Amana Colonies. Enjoy your visit!

Opportunities for Visitors

One might describe the Amana Colonies as a collection of quaint villages offering good food and many shopping opportunities. While that would be true, the seven villages offer much more to visitors.

The Amana Colonies are the largest tourist attraction in Iowa, with the number of visitors approaching 1.5 million per year. Ever since Church members arrived in Iowa in 1855 to build these communities, people have been curious about the Amana Colonies. Visitors have wondered what life is like in these communities and have wanted a firsthand look at how the people live, work, play, and pray. While many things have changed since the days of the communal society, many others are still the same.

Amana is a wholesome place, with friendly people, safe streets, bountiful restaurants, warm, homey, bed and breakfast inns, and dozens of charming shops offering a wide variety of gifts and other items.

For many tourists, the Amana Colonies may be most famous for their food. The Colonies have nine restaurants, and there are three more at the Little Amana interstate complex. Most of the restaurants serve abundant, family-style meals, with refillable plates and bowls of food brought to the table to be passed around for enjoyment. No one ever leaves an Amana restaurant hungry.

While restaurants in the Amana Colonies have long been famous, a relatively new growth in bed and breakfast inns has given visitors an opportunity to stay overnight in the villages, often in old homes which were used in the communal days as kitchen houses or residential homes. There are nine inns in the Colonies and two more near the Little Amana interstate complex. Eleven other lodging facilities are also available at or near the Little Amana interstate complex.

The Amana Colonies offer visitors opportunities to shop for a wide range of products, including antiques, arts and crafts, handcrafted furniture, woolen products, Christmas items, aged wine and cheese, microbrewery products, and homemade candy, bread, and pastries. A subject index at the end of this guide will help direct visitors to all of these shops and other businesses.

The Amana Colonies of today have not forgotten their past. Efforts have been underway for several decades to preserve the heritage of the communities. Today, these efforts are evident in a number of well-managed museums. Artifacts are seen throughout the villages, and the preservation of buildings in their original exterior condition is common. Various publications are available concerning the Colonies, and a listing of many of these can be found in the final chapter.

The Colonies also offer outdoor activities, including an 18-hole professional golf course; a nature trail which leads to an old Native American fishing dam on the Iowa River; historic, peaceful cemeteries; and a lake which blossoms each summer with brilliant lilies.

The Colonies are easily accessible by automobile on the Amana Colonies Trail, a highway network which connects all seven villages to Interstate 80. For those who prefer to tour on foot, a walking tour of Amana is available through the Amana Heritage Society, and self-guided walking tours of several of the other villages are also offered. For the benefit of bicyclists, an effort is underway to provide bicycle paths in and around the villages.

ANNUAL EVENTS IN THE AMANA COLONIES

Contact the Amana Colonies Convention and Visitors Bureau for more information on the following yearly events.

Maifest—first weekend of May in Amana, a celebration of spring with a parade, food fair, crafts, and special events.
Antique marble show—early June, held at the Little Amana interstate complex.
Splinterfest—third weekend of June at the Amana Farmer's Market, woodcrafts.
Minneapolis-Moline implement reunion—third weekend of June in Homestead, antique farm equipment and parade.
Flea market—last weekend in June, Amana Colonies Convention and Visitors Bureau.
Bluegrass festival—middle of July, music festival in Middle Amana at the Amana Community Park.

Amana festival of the arts—second Saturday in August, various arts, crafts, and entertainment in Middle Amana at the Amana Community Park.

Tanager Place summerfest—middle of August in Amana, various events and balloon festival for youth organization.

Holzfest—third weekend of August, Iowa's biggest woodcraft show, Little Amana interstate complex.

Oktoberfest—first weekend of October in Amana, fall harvest celebration with parade, art and craft demonstrations, and entertainment.

Midwest fall fibre show—first weekend of November at the Amana Arts Guild Center in High Amana, fiber media works including weaving, baskets, quilts, and textiles.

Prelude to Christmas—first weekend of December in Amana, village-wide holiday celebration with Santa, decorations, candlelit streets, Christmas cookie walk, and a Christmas-past exhibit at the Museum of Amana History.

ART AND CRAFT DEMONSTRATIONS

A number of demonstrations are offered in the villages at existing businesses, museums, and the Amana Arts Guild Center, and during various arts festivals held in the Colonies. Check with the Amana Arts Guild Center or the specific business for demonstration times, and refer to the listing under each chapter.

Amana Arts Guild Center—High Amana, various demonstrations

Amana Furniture Shop—Amana, woodworking

Amana Woolen Mill—Amana, operating woolen looms

Fenn Works—Amana, glassblowing

Colony Candle—Amana, candle making

Krauss Furniture Shop—South Amana, woodworking

Museum of Amana History—Amana, various demonstrations

Powder House—Amana, woodworking

Roger's Anvil/Old Machine Shop Museum—Amana, blacksmith

Schanz Broom and Basket—Amana, basket making
Schanz Broom and Basket—West Amana, broom making
Schanz Furniture Shop—South Amana, woodworking

Definition of Terms

Several terms used in this guide and within the villages may require a definition. More specific information can be found in the next section under "Amana History" or within other entries.

■ General Amana Terms

Amana—A biblical phrase meaning "believe faithfully." It is also the name given to the first and main village in Iowa settled by the Community of True Inspiration in 1855.
Amana Colonies—A reference to the seven villages which were settled by the Community of True Inspiration.
Amana Church Society—The name given to the religious organization of the Community of True Inspiration after the Great Change of 1932.
Amana Heritage Society—An organization created to preserve the cultural heritage of the seven villages. It collects and preserves items of historical significance and manages several museums within the Colonies.
Amana Society—The name for the incorporated seven villages of the Amana Colonies. In 1932, this entity became a for-profit corporation and today operates a large farming enterprise, some real estate ventures, and several businesses and shops.
Amish—A group of German immigrants who settled in Kalona, Iowa, about the same time Amana was being settled. Although they appear to have similarities to the Amana people, there is no connection between the two groups, and Amish people do not live in Amana.
Calico mill—A factory which produced colored fabrics for use and sale. It existed in the Colonies until World War I, when German dyes became unavailable.

Colony—Refers to the seven villages as a whole.

Communal—Collective ownership and use of property by a group or community. Amana was a communal society, and everything was owned and shared equally among all members.

Communal kitchen houses—Eating houses, a number of which were located in each village and which provided all the meals for the villagers. Members generally received their meals under this system until the Great Change of 1932.

Communal residence—Individual homes in the villages. Homes were often occupied by extended families, including children, parents, and grandparents. Sometimes more than one family shared a home.

Communal society—A social/economic system in which the members of a community agree to share all ownership and use of property among themselves.

Community of True Inspiration—The name of a Christian religious movement, created in 1714, which practices the teachings of Jesus Christ and believes that God speaks to people through *Werkzeuge*, or inspired leaders. The Community made its way to New York in 1843 and to Amana, Iowa, in 1855.

Ebenezer—A biblical phrase meaning "hitherto hath the Lord helped us." It is the name the Community of True Inspiration gave to their first village established in America, near Buffalo, New York.

Great Change—Refers to the time in 1932 when members of the seven villages voted to abandon their communal system in favor of the capitalist system. The Community vested all its property in the Amana Society, which issued stock to village members. The religious aspects of the Community were vested in the Amana Church Society.

Kinderschule—Children's school. This was the day care operation in the villages. Children stayed with their mother until age two and then went to *Kinderschule* while the mother returned to work.

Kitchen boss—An appointed female head of the communal kitchen operation. Each village had several kitchen houses, with a separate boss, *Küchebaas*, for each house. This was an important position in the villages.

Little Amana—A tourist stop along Interstate 80 which features several restaurants, shops, and lodging facilities. Little Amana is not part of the Amana Colonies.

Millrace—A seven-mile canal dug by the villagers in the 1860s to provide power for various mills.

Saal—A meeting room. The church in each village was called the *Saal*.

Werkzeuge—Inspired ones. A *Werkzeug* was an inspired leader of the Community, much like a prophet, who provided direction for spiritual and community affairs. The Community believed the *Werkzeug* was someone who was directly inspired by God.

A History of the Amana Colonies

■ Historic Overview

The Amana Colonies are seven villages in Iowa County, Iowa, which were settled as a communal religious society by European immigrants who came to America in 1843 seeking greater religious freedom and more promising economic opportunities. Amana is a biblical phrase from the Song of Solomon meaning "believe faithfully."

Amana has its roots in the Pietist religious movement of eighteenth-century Germany, where some Christians had grown unhappy with the direction of the Lutheran Church, particularly with its dogmatism and its intellectualization of religion to the detriment of personal religious needs.

The leaders of one particular movement were Johann Friedrich Rock (1678–1749) and Eberhard Ludwig Gruber (1665–1728), who founded the Community of True Inspiration in Himbach, Germany, in 1714. Rooted in the Bible and the teachings of Jesus Christ, the newly founded group sought a belief system that focused on the personal experience of religion. The group believed that certain leaders were inspired by God to provide direction and purpose to individuals' lives. When these leaders spoke as *Werkzeuge* (inspired ones), their words were recorded as testimonials. Rock provided testimonies to his followers for 35 years, until his death.

The movement spurned the government's expectations of military duty and schooling for their youth. Consequently, members were persecuted with fines, imprisonment, and physical beatings.

After Rock and Gruber died, the movement faded until 1817, when Michael Krausert helped revive the Community with the help of Christian Metz and Barbara Heinemann. The movement began to flourish, particularly among the peasants and craftspeople in Germany, Alsace, and Switzerland, many of whom had suffered because of war, famine, and the European industrial movement. As the group continued to grow, it found sanctuary in various castles in the German province of Hesse-Darmstadt. Heinemann and Metz both became *Werkzeuge*, and Metz became the leader of the group during the 1820s.

By 1840, the Community had 1,000 members but was frustrated by increased living costs, several droughts, and continued persecution. In 1842, Christian Metz and three others set sail for America to find land for a new community. They purchased 5,000 acres of the Seneca Indian Reservation near Buffalo, New York, and proceeded to move 800 members to the new community they called Ebenezer, a biblical phrase meaning "hitherto hath the Lord helped us." Six villages were constructed (in a system similar to that used later in Amana), 4,000 more acres were purchased, and the population grew to 1,200.

As nearby Buffalo continued to grow, the villagers felt the pressure of the outside world. Land prices increased, goods from Buffalo created competition for village goods, and unwanted contact with outsiders pressured the religious community. Therefore, in 1854, the group decided to move west.

Scouts had liked a location in the fertile Iowa River Valley, with its rich, productive soil, strong limestone and sandstone quarry inventory, and abundant timber. These resources, as well as Iowa's relative isolation as a newly developing territory, made the location ideal. Construction began in the village of Amana in 1855.

Over the next 10 years, as Ebenezer property was sold, the Community members moved to Amana. By 1862, all seven of the Amana villages had been established, and the group had been incorporated as the Amana Society. The villages were all located within a six-mile radius so that the agricultural enterprise could be managed efficiently. The order in which the villages were established was Amana, 1855; West Amana, 1856; South Amana, 1856; High Amana, 1857; Homestead, purchased in 1860; East Amana, 1860; and Middle Amana, 1862.

The villages flourished, creating a vast farming and gardening operation to provide food and work for members; lumberyards and stone quarries to provide building materials for homes; business operations, including a series of trade shops to produce necessary goods and services such as baskets, furniture, and wagons, and woolen and calico mills which produced products for both internal use and external sale.

These external sales provided funds to assist in managing the villages. They also helped build Amana's reputation as a producer of quality products. The farms produced a wide range of grains and vegetables and sold excess onions in Chicago for additional income.

The villages were laid out in the German style, with one long street and few side streets. Most of the agricultural buildings were clustered at one end of town, the craft shops and any factories at the other. On either side were the spacious gardens, orchards, and vineyards. Homes and community kitchens were located in the middle of the villages. The church was placed in the center of each village.

Good land was used for agricultural purposes, lesser land for building homes. Each village had between 40 and 100 homes and a number of shops. Homes were typically plain, square, two-story, gable-roof structures made from wood, sandstone, or brick. No paint was applied to the wood structures because rebuilding was less expensive than painting. Trellises were common on homes and provided shade as well as a crop of grapes or roses. Large, beautiful flower beds with dozens of varieties were planted around the homes and meticulously tended.

A *Saal*, or church, and schools were located in each village. The usual shops included a bakery, blacksmith, broom and basket shop, carpenter, cooper or tinsmith, dairy operation, fire station, general store, grain house, harness maker, meat shop, locksmith, post office, printer, shoemaker, tailor, wagon maker, watchmaker, waterworks, and wine cellar.

Some villages also had a woolen mill, calico mill, depot, lumberyard, doctor, and pharmacy. To power the mill operations, the community built a millrace. The millrace was a seven-mile-long canal, dug out using oxen first, and then dredging boats built by the villagers. The millrace tapped into the Iowa River and traveled through Middle Amana and Amana before reconnecting to the Iowa River.

The farming operations planted corn, oats, barley, rye, potatoes, and onions. They raised beef cattle, dairy cattle, hogs, and sheep, and kept apiaries for honey. The communal kitchen operation kept hens and chickens for eggs and meat, and planted beans, beets, cabbage, herbs, garlic, leeks, lettuce, pumpkins, squash, tomatoes, and other vegetables. The communities produced shoes, watches, lamps, soap, cigars, beer, and wine for members.

Every member of the Community was provided a home, food, medical care, education, and a job. Cash was not exchanged. Each member was given a yearly allowance to be redeemed at the general store or other shops for personal items. In return, the members worked and abided by the rules of the Community. Outsiders were allowed to join the Community if they contributed their belongings, signed an oath, and confessed their sins. Members were free to leave the Community at any time, and while a few did, most seemed to be content with their faith and their Colony.

After the deaths of Christian Metz, in 1867, and Barbara Heinemann (now Barbara Heinemann Landmann), in 1883, no inspired leaders remained in the Community. At this point, the strong religious authority of the church began to slowly decline. This decline in church authority combined with the difficult economic conditions of early twentieth-century America and an increasing lack of isolation from the outside world placed the Community on a path toward transition.

When new railroads began to sprout around the state, Iowa became more densely populated until the outside world was at Amana's door. The introduction of new items such as radios, automobiles, and shopping catalogs and the persistent effect of newspapers, music, and modern dress continued to place the Community at odds with the outside world and began to drive a wedge between generations within the Colonies.

On the economic side, higher taxes, inflation, and an increasing dependence on outside labor pressed the Colonies' resources. Some members had begun selling products or services to the outside world for individual profit. Others were becoming lazy, while a few simply refused to work. A few members appeared to have stolen outright from the Community. These problems, which created disparities among villagers, were upsetting the integrity of the communal way of life.

Members also began skipping church services. The young frequently skipped Saturday night and other evening services. Barring members from church services, which had been an effective control mechanism under Metz's leadership, began to be viewed as a blessing rather than as a punishment by members who had grown weary of the high number of church services and the rigidity of the Community's rules.

In 1923, a devastating explosion and subsequent fire destroyed the flour mill and damaged the woolen mill in Amana. In all, 13 buildings were destroyed and nearly $500,000 in damage occurred. The Society had no insurance. They had believed it was more economical to rebuild lost buildings using their resources and labor than it was to buy insurance. This disaster contributed to the Community's growing economic plight.

Increasingly, the Amana Colonies seemed to be faced with a decision. Either they had to abandon the outside world and return to their ancestors' ways, which meant becoming more strict with members, or they had to join the modern world, shifting from communalism to capitalism.

After the need for change became more widely recognized and accepted within the villages, the Society developed a plan for severing their economic bonds and moving to a capitalist system. Eventually, village members voted overwhelmingly to make the transition, and in May 1932, the old Society ceased to exist and a new corporation, also known as the Amana Society, was formed. This landmark became known as the Great Change.

Before the Great Change, the Community had functioned successfully as a communal group for 89 years. Much of the credit for this longevity can be assigned to factors such as the strong, inspired leadership of Christian Metz, the deeply held and shared religious beliefs of the Community, and the vigorous and diversified economic structure of the Community.

After the Great Change, religious affairs became the exclusive domain of the Amana Church Society, and the business enterprises were handled by the new Amana Society. All members of the Community were issued stock in the corporation based on their age and years of service to the Community. In turn, members could use this stock to purchase homes or property or to obtain cash. The Society would manage the farms, mills, shops, and other business enterprises and share the profits with the stockholders. Many shops were closed or consolidated with shops in other villages, and members were offered jobs in the remaining shops or on the farms. In May 1932, the Society issued $1.7 million in stock to its members. At that time, community assets totaled over $2.7 million with liabilities of $500,000. The people of Amana began a new way of life, and the Community of True Inspiration began a new chapter in its long history.

Today, the Amana Church Society is still in existence and has a strong and devoted membership. The Amana Society continues to operate businesses within the Colonies and manages the largest farming operation in Iowa. Furthermore, tourism has become a giant industry in Amana, as visitors seek to learn about the history of this unique community and enjoy its fine restaurants, shops, and historical displays.

In 1965, the Amana Colonies were added to the National Register of Historic Places as a National Historic Landmark. Today, the villages have historic inventories approaching 1,000 buildings.

Throughout most of the communal years, the population of the seven villages ranged between 1,370 and 1,770. Today, village population is around 1,700.

■ Life and Customs in the Colonies

■ RELIGIOUS BELIEFS

Central to any understanding of the Amana Colonies is the extremely strong influence of religion. Religious beliefs and the need to practice them freely were the genesis of the Community.

The Church of the Community of True Inspiration is a Christian movement with a strong belief in the Bible and the original teachings of Jesus Christ. The Inspirationists believe that God speaks through *Werkzeuge*, or inspired leaders, who provide direction, admonitions, and purpose to the Community. The Community had two sets of guiding rules: The 24 Rules of True Godliness, which was an ethical code, and The 21 Rules for the Examination of Daily Life, which focused on spiritual devotion.

The church *Saal*, or meeting room, was built in the center of each village, an appropriate place since faith was the center of the Community. There were no altars, statues, decorative stained-glass windows, or steeples, but rather the church was a typical village building with simple, blue-colored walls and plain wooden benches. Men and women entered and sat on separate sides of the *Saal*. Men wore suits to the *Saal*, and women wore black dresses with black aprons and black shawls or caps. Members brought their Bibles, testimonial books with readings from the *Werkzeug*, and hymnbooks. Several Church elders presided at the service.

The Church had three general levels of piety, and some separate services were held throughout the week for each level. Elders decided in which level a member would be placed, and the bases for distinction included age, marital status, and Church attendance, with celibacy and regular Church attendance being given the greatest weight. The level of piety a member attained would also dictate where he or she sat: the higher the level of piety, the farther back in the *Saal* one could sit.

Children under age 15 attended a separate service, without their parents, although some parents might be assigned to the children's level, depending on their standing in the Church.

The Church had 11 meetings per week, ranging from short evening prayer meetings to longer services on Sunday. The meetings included evening prayer meetings each day, afternoon services on Wednesday, Saturday, and Sunday, and a morning service on Sunday.

Members could be admonished or demoted by Church elders as punishment for various transgressions such as breaking Community rules or missing services. Punishments included having to sit toward the front of the Church, being sent to the children's service, or being banished from services for a specified time. The Church practiced an in-depth confession each year and a communion and foot-washing ceremony commemorating Jesus Christ every other year.

Today, all of the faithful attend the same service, which is held once a week at the church in Middle Amana. There are two Sunday services, one in German and one in English. The church in Amana is also used for various services or special occasions. The strict control of the Church has been lost, but the members are strong in their faith, continuing the tradition created by Rock and Gruber in 1714.

■ POLITICAL AUTHORITY

In both Ebenezer and Amana, the Community drafted a constitution, and members pledged to abide by the constitution in order to join. Those wishing to join were required to contribute all of their money and possessions in return for full membership rights. Members were also free to leave the Community at any time and have their contributions returned, but few ever left.

The seven villages were run by a great council which included representatives from each village. Each village had at least one member, and the total council consisted of 13 members, the number representing Christ and his 12 apostles. The council was elected annually by all eligible voting members in the Colonies. This included all male members over age 21 and all women over 30 not already represented by a male vote.

While Christian Metz was living, he held a high level of authority over the Community because of his status as an instrument of God (*Werkzeug*). Metz was consulted by the great council on important matters and provided guidance in all areas. After his death, the council elected a director, a vice-director, and a secretary.

In addition to the great council, each village had its own council of elders which managed the affairs of the individual village. These councils directed members to work assignments, managed the business operations, determined allowances, and approved couples for marriage, for example. This group could vary in size from 6 to 18. A head elder presided over this group in each of the villages.

Another level of elders directed Church activities in each village. There was a head elder for each *Saal*. In addition to the elders, the farm managers, business managers, and communal kitchen house bosses wielded a considerable amount of authority in their villages.

After the Great Change in 1932, this system of authority no longer existed.

■ EDUCATION

Amana students were always busy learning at school. They went to class six days a week, up to 50 weeks a year.

The daytime instruction was divided into three phases. The morning was spent covering material such as reading, writing, and arithmetic, as well as learning English and German. There was then a lengthy recess time which focused on play and exercise. The afternoon was devoted to manual training and instruction in various trades. One such trade was knitting, and both boys and girls learned to knit and made their own winter stockings.

Schoolchildren planted and maintained school gardens, and

The Homestead school circa 1910. Amana students went to school six days a week, up to 50 weeks a year. (Photo courtesy Amana Heritage Society.)

they were also responsible for the village orchards. Each year, school would be suspended for a period of time up to two weeks while the students harvested fruit from the orchards.

Amana schools have always been accredited in the Iowa public school system. Since their school day was longer and they met on Saturdays, they used this extra time for religious instruction. The teachers lived in the villages but had instruction outside the community at various institutions of higher education.

Children started school at age five and went year-round until age 14. When their studies were completed, the students graduated after an examination by the village elders, the recitation of a composition regarding their educational focus, and a reading from an essay about their life aspirations. After graduating, children were assigned a trade or apprenticeship, in accordance with their interests and skills and the needs of the village. Some students were sent outside the community to colleges or universities to receive instruction in medicine or education. The Society

Boys harvesting apples, circa 1903. Schoolchildren were responsible for the village orchards and were excused from school at harvesttime. (Photo courtesy Amana Heritage Society.)

paid for this education, and the students later returned to put their new skills to use.

Today, Amana students are part of a consolidated rural school district. Instruction and activities are like those in any other public school in Iowa.

■ WORK AND TRADES

Everyone in the Community was expected to work and did so. Depending on the season, workdays began between 6:30 am and 7:00 am and lasted until 6:00 pm, with several meal and snack breaks. A wide variety of jobs existed in the villages. Older members were generally assigned lighter tasks. Women typically worked in the communal kitchen system, which required a large workforce. Women were also caregivers for the children, handled the laundry, and took care of sewing and knitting projects. A few women worked in the woolen mills.

Men worked in the farming operation, one of the mills, or one of the many trades available. Many youths would continue their family tradition in a particular line of work. A baker's son would become a baker, a blacksmith's son would become a blacksmith, or a kitchen boss's daughter would work in the communal kitchen house. But young people did have choices and could request work assignments in areas of interest or particular talent.

The members were not paid cash, but received an education, home, food, medical care, and an annual allowance at the general store and shops in the village to purchase personal items.

Mothers with newborn children were excused from work for two years so they could stay at home and care for their babies. When children turned age two, they were taken to the *Kinderschule*, or day care, and the mother returned to her work assignment.

Today village residents have jobs like anyone else. Some are employed by the Amana Society.

■ COMMUNITY KITCHEN HOUSES

Each village had a number of community kitchen houses, each providing meals for around 40 members. Members were assigned to kitchen houses and came there for the five daily meals that were provided. New mothers and members who were ill had their food delivered. For several years before the Great Change of 1932, some people would come to the kitchen, pick up the food, and take it home.

A female kitchen boss, selected by the village elders, ran the kitchen operation. She and her family lived in the adjoining house. This position was one of the most important in the village. The boss had an assistant and, usually, three women who worked in the kitchen and rotated the chores of preparing vegetables, cooking, and washing dishes.

The vast kitchen gardens that provided the vegetables were a critical area, and a garden boss managed this operation. Tending the fields, harvesting, and drying and canning fruits and vegetables was a major undertaking and was essential to the smooth operation of the community.

Each day, the local bakery would deliver bread, the local meat

Women at work in a communal kitchen house. Around 40 villagers were assigned to a kitchen house, where they ate all their meals. (Photo courtesy Amana Heritage Society.)

Amana women sorting onions, Homestead circa 1890s. Work was a joint effort in the villages. (Photo courtesy Amana Heritage Society.)

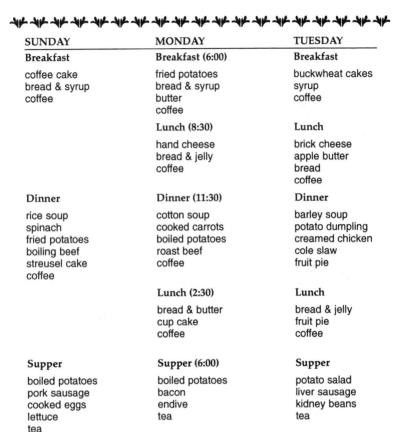

SUNDAY	MONDAY	TUESDAY
Breakfast	**Breakfast (6:00)**	**Breakfast**
coffee cake	fried potatoes	buckwheat cakes
bread & syrup	bread & syrup	syrup
coffee	butter	coffee
	coffee	
	Lunch (8:30)	**Lunch**
	hand cheese	brick cheese
	bread & jelly	apple butter
	coffee	bread
		coffee
Dinner	**Dinner (11:30)**	**Dinner**
rice soup	cotton soup	barley soup
spinach	cooked carrots	potato dumpling
fried potatoes	boiled potatoes	creamed chicken
boiling beef	roast beef	cole slaw
streusel cake	coffee	fruit pie
coffee		
	Lunch (2:30)	**Lunch**
	bread & butter	bread & jelly
	cup cake	fruit pie
	coffee	coffee
Supper	**Supper (6:00)**	**Supper**
boiled potatoes	boiled potatoes	potato salad
pork sausage	bacon	liver sausage
cooked eggs	endive	kidney beans
lettuce	tea	tea
tea		

A typical weekly menu from a communal kitchen house. The menu might vary depending on the season and availability of food. (Menu courtesy Robert Trumpold from How It Was in the Communal Kitchen, *by Marie Trumpold Geiger and Jonathan Andelson.)*

shop would deliver the necessary fresh meat, and the dairy would drop off milk and butter. The kitchen boss managed all of these matters and kept financial accounts of items and supplies used by the kitchen, ranging from sugar and milk to kettles and knives.

During the winter months, ice was harvested from the Iowa River, the Homestead Pond, and the Lily Lake between Amana and Middle Amana. The ice was packed in sawdust and stored

WEDNESDAY	THURSDAY	FRIDAY	SATURDAY
Breakfast	**Breakfast**	**Breakfast**	**Breakfast**
potatoes bread & butter coffee	oatmeal bread & butter syrup coffee	fried potatoes bread & butter coffee	fried potatoes bread & butter syrup coffee
Lunch	**Lunch**	**Lunch**	**Lunch**
hand cheese bread onion pie coffee	rolls brick cheese coffee	brick cheese bread & jelly coffee	cheese bread & jelly coffee
Dinner	**Dinner**	**Dinner**	**Dinner**
potato soup boiled cabbage french fries boiling beef pudding bread coffee	pea soup filled noodles lettuce applesauce cinnamon rolls coffee	crumb soup sauerkraut spareribs potatoes starch pudding coffee	tomato soup potatoes sauerkraut eggs coffee cake
Lunch	**Lunch**	**Lunch**	**Lunch**
bread & jelly pudding coffee	bread & jelly kolaches coffee	bread & jelly coffee	bread & jelly coffee
Supper	**Supper**	**Supper**	**Supper**
hamburger frenchstyle beans mash potatoes tea	roast pork potatoes red cabbage tea	stew potatoes tomatoes tea	boiled potatoes cottage cheese cheese spread tea

in ice houses, which were built with 16-inch-thick walls. This method ensured a supply of ice to the kitchen houses throughout the summer months.

Depending on the season, breakfast was served at 6:00 am or 6:30 am, dinner at 11:30 am, and supper usually at 6:00 pm. Men and women sat at separate tables, there was little talking during meals, and a prayer opened and closed each meal. A midmorning and a midafternoon lunch were also served, usually cheese, breads, and coffee for the morning lunch and dessert and coffee for the afternoon lunch. During planting and harvesting times, these meals were often delivered to field workers.

Due to the planning involved in such an undertaking, the menus at the community kitchens tended to remain the same. There were 33 weekly meals provided (only three on Sundays because there was no work). Although menu items might change due to supply and seasonal variety, the schedule remained fairly consistent.

Washhouses and woodsheds were near the kitchen houses for cleaning and to supply wood for the oven. Chicken houses were also nearby to supply eggs.

After the Great Change in 1932, the communal kitchen house era ended. Families had to install kitchen areas in existing homes because only the kitchen houses had originally been built with kitchens.

At times, the Amana Heritage Society offers an opportunity to eat an authentic meal in the Communal Kitchen Museum in Middle Amana. Check with the Museum or the Amana Heritage Society for possible opportunities.

■ RECREATION

The villages had many recreational activities and celebrations for entertainment. Birthdays and holidays were celebrated as were religious events and weddings.

The nearby millrace and Iowa River provided opportunities for fishing and swimming in the summer and for ice skating parties in the winter. The forests were used for walks, hiking, and picnics. Beautiful pine groves existed in the villages and provided a tranquil environment for villagers. Young people often gathered at one of the three train depots, the kitchen houses, or the schools. Wednesday and Saturday nights were designated "date nights" for young people. Although baseball was a forbidden pastime in the Colonies, boys would sneak off to play the game. After 1900, baseball games became more common in some of the villages.

Until 1884, when an Iowa prohibition law went into effect, beer was made throughout the villages and enjoyed by mem-

Friends at a birthday party for Elizabeth Eichacker—in the white cap—Homestead, circa 1915. (Photo courtesy Amana Heritage Society.)

A family picnic near Homestead, circa 1915. Picnics, fishing, and ice skating were popular forms of recreation. (Photo courtesy Amana Heritage Society.)

bers. Prohibition effectively ended the art of beer making in the Colonies, and villagers purchased beer from other sources when it again became legal.

Wine was also enjoyed by the Colonists, who brought their extensive wine-making skills from Germany. The basement of the Church building was used as a wine cellar, and each member was given a punch ticket and an allotment of wine each year. In 1919, when prohibition was enacted throughout America, the Colonists complied, dumping several thousand gallons of wine into the nearby river. They joked that every catfish from Amana to Louisiana had a hangover the next day. After prohibition ended, the wine-making industry was revived. Today nine wineries operate in the Colonies.

■ Marriage

To be married in the villages, females had to be 21 and males 24. Members who wished to marry presented themselves to the village elders and sought permission to be wed. If permission was given, a wedding date was set for the following year. In the early days of the Community, the two young people were separated for one year, as a test of their intentions. One member was moved to another village, and the two young people were allowed to see one another only twice a week. The two members spent the year of separation preparing for the wedding: the women crafted various household items, and the men prepared beer and wine for the wedding celebration. Later this practice was halted.

Marriage ceremonies were simple. Usually only relatives attended. There were no rings or flowers at the ceremony. The women wore the same black attire worn to other church services. Following the service, there was a large celebration to which villagers were invited. Food, wine, beer, and an array of cakes were served, and guests sang and played games. The newlyweds spent the first week after their marriage with their families and were then assigned to a home.

Celibacy was encouraged over marriage, particularly in the earlier years of the Community. For those that did marry, the average family included two children. These marriage customs ended with the Great Change of 1932.

■ DEATH

The death of a village member was treated as a solemn and religious experience. Grieving occurred, but stoic behavior was preferred.

If the member died at home, the clock in the room was stopped at the time of death. The village cabinetmaker was called, and he carefully measured the body so that no material would be wasted in constructing the coffin. The deceased was dressed in white rather than the usual black church attire, and viewing took place in the member's home. A vigil was kept by family and friends, with someone always in attendance. Ice was used to preserve the body. Burial occurred on the third day, signifying the resurrection of Jesus Christ.

On the day of the burial, a service was held, and there was an elaborate procession to the village cemetery, where the individual was buried. Nearly all members were buried in the order of death rather than in family plots. A simple, rounded, white headstone marked each grave with a name, date of death, and usually the member's age in years, months, and days.

On the following day, the viewing room was cleaned to remove all traces of death.

Funeral customs have changed since the Great Change of 1932, although residents are still buried in the village cemeteries.

Amana

Amana was the first and the largest of the seven villages settled by the Community of True Inspiration after they began their move from Ebenezer, New York, to Iowa in 1855. The name Amana is a biblical phrase from the Song of Solomon meaning believe faithfully. For a more detailed history of the Amana Colonies, please refer to the previous chapter.

Today, Amana is still the largest of the seven villages and offers visitors a wide array of restaurants, shops, and activities. The village has five restaurants, all run by families with Amana heritage. Food is also available in a sit-down setting at the Amana Stone Hearth Bakery, the Colony Cone, and the Village Pastry Shop. A number of shops offer other food items such as fudge, candy, breads, jams and jellies, sauerkraut, and noodles.

Amana has two lodging facilities, an expansive park for recreational vehicles and conventions, and 60 shops and tourist attractions including furniture and craft shops, antique and Christmas stores, several wineries, a microbrewery, and a museum filled with historical and educational information about the Colonies.

Construction of Amana began in 1855, when a group of 33 Inspirationists arrived from the Ebenezer Colony in New York and began building. Amana was constructed in the German tradition, with one long street and several side streets. The farm buildings were at one end of the street and the essential shops at the other end. On either side of these were the orchards and gardens. The schools were near the fruit orchard. The church, 16 communal kitchen houses, and the communal residences were in the center of the town. The homes and buildings were connected by a pathway of narrow planks. These were replaced by narrow concrete sidewalks around 1900.

Amana Colonies Guide

Amana
1. Lily Lake
2. Amana Colonies Visitors Center
3. Amana Colonies Convention and Visitors Bureau
4. Old Creamery Theatre Company
5. Colony Visits/Heritage Destinations
6. Amana Colonies RV Park
7. Colony Cone
8. Antiques and Things
9. Smokehouse Square Antiques
10. Amana Meat Shop and Smokehouse
11. Grape Vine Winery and Gift Shop
12. Erenberger Antiques
13. Renate's Antique Gallery
14. Village Pastry Shop
15. Der Weinkeller
16. Powder House
17. Antique Tower Haus
18. Colony Candleworks
19. Village Mall
20. Village Leather Haus
21. Old Wine Cellar Winery
22. Lehm Books and Gifts
23. Old World Lace Shoppe
24. Santa's Sleigh
25. Amana General Store
26. Sandstone Winery
27. Heritage Designs Needlework and Quilting
28. Oma's Haus
29. Carole's Giftshop
30. Amana Handimart
31. Nordy's Subs & Salads
32. Museum of Amana History
33. Heritage Wine and Cheese Haus
34. Ronneburg Restaurant
35. Colony Gardens
36. Clothes Encounter
37. Ox Yoke Inn
38. Tick Tock Antiques
39. Noé House Inn
40. Red Geranium
41. Gingerbread House
42. The Christmas Room
43. Oak Ridge Gallery
44. Amana Stone Hearth Bakery
45. Great Midwest Leather
46. Creative Colony
47. Tiny Tim's Colony Christmas
48. Amana Farmer's Market
49. Amana Barn Restaurant

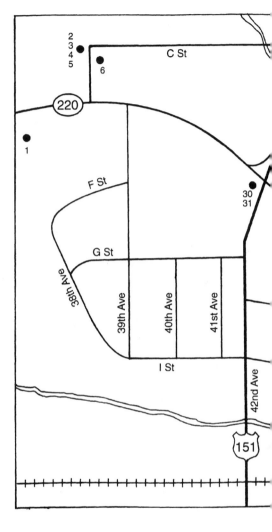

Amana

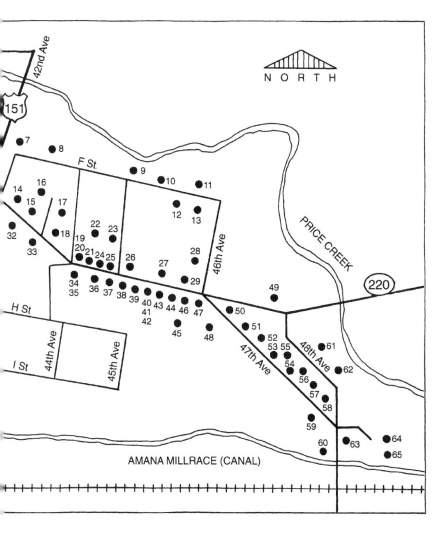

50. Broom and Basket Shop
51. Country Connection
52. Guest House Motel
53. Brick Haus Restaurant
54. Maddie's/Der Laden Apparel and Gifts
55. Red Fox Paper Den
56. Colony Inn Candy Store
57. Schnitzelbank
58. Kitchen Sink
59. Colony Inn Restaurant
60. Millstream Brewing Company
61. Amana Furniture Shop
62. Village Winery and Gift Gallery
63. Amana Woolen Mill
64. Fenn Works
65. Roger's Anvil/ Industrial Machine Shop Museum

Map numbers also appear beside the description of each establishment.

Three women hoe a garden in East Amana, August 1937. Large gardens provided the bulk of the food for the villagers. (Photo by John Barry, courtesy Amana Heritage Society.)

The shops and buildings of the community included an ash house, bakery, bookbindery, blacksmith, boat house (for the millrace dredge boat), buggy shed, butcher shop, carpenter, carpet weaver, cooper or tinsmith, dentist, depot, doctor, fire station, harness maker, hobo shack, hotel, general store, icehouse, locksmith and machine shop, lumber shed, pharmacy, pump house, press house, tailor, sawmill, shoemaker, wagon shop, and watch house.

In addition to these, there were several factory and agricultural buildings in Amana. The factories included a calico mill, cereal mill, flour mill, and woolen mill. The agricultural buildings included apiaries, calf barns, a cattle barn, dairy barn, granary, hog powder house (where a livestock feed additive was produced), horse and colt barn, machine shed, oxen and steer barn, and a shed for a stationary threshing machine.

Restaurants

■ Amana Barn Restaurant [49]*

■ QUICK FACTS
Telephone: 319-622-3214/800-325-2045
Hours: Mon–Thu 11:00 am–8:30 pm, Fri–Sat 11:00 am–9:00 pm, Sun 11:00 am–8:00 pm, Sunday brunch 10:00 am–1:00 pm
Capacity: 360
Groups: yes
Parking: spacious lot, RVs welcome
Handicap accessible: yes
Smoking: in designated area only
Price range: lunch platters $6.95–$9.95, sandwiches $5.75–$7.25, lunch and dinner entrees $9.95–$14.75
Payment methods: cash, check, American Express, Discover, MasterCard, Visa

The Amana Barn Restaurant has a hefty American beef menu in addition to traditional German fare. (Photo by author.)

---

* The number refers to location on the village map.

Family-style dining: yes
Children's menu: yes
Customer favorites: Sunday brunch and prime rib au jus served with champagne mustard
Building: constructed 1983 as a restaurant
Restaurant opened: 1983
Hosts: Harold and Helen Schuerer and their children, Neal Schuerer and Carol Schuerer Zuber

The Amana Barn Restaurant has added top quality Iowa beef products to a menu respectful of the German tradition; it offers diners a wide selection of menu items.

The restaurant was built on the site of an old 1865 cattle barn. Some of the materials from the barn were used in the new building, and it is designed like an old barn, complete with cupolas. The lofting shed is the entry foyer and includes a lounge and a small gift area. The Barn's spacious Hunter's Trophy Lounge features displays of various stuffed wildlife, a television, and a full-service bar. The building has a sandstone and wood exterior with exposed beams on the inside.

The Barn is operated by the Harold Schuerer family. Harold and his wife Helen started the business in 1983. Their son, Neal Schuerer, and daughter, Carole Schuerer Zuber, manage the day-to-day operations of the restaurant.

Harold's family has a long history in the food business, including working in the meat shop and kitchen houses during communal days. Harold's brother Walter operates the nearby Brick Haus restaurant. Another brother, George, operates the Grape Vine Winery and Gift Shop.

The popular prime rib, as well as the long list of other beef items, is one of the reasons the Barn was awarded the Iowa Beef Council's 1996 Beef Backer Award. The Beef Council indicated they were recognizing the Barn's superior use of beef products, particularly those with an accent on German-flavored dishes.

The German tradition lives on at the Barn, which offers a full selection of German specialties. Many guests like to try the Variety Sampler, which comes with two or three meats and family-style side dishes. Another favorite is the *Rouladen*. It is thinly sliced round steak topped with German mustard, chopped onion, carrots, and dill pickle, then slowly braised and served with homemade potato dumplings.

The Barn serves warm bread and offers interesting side dishes such as pickled baby carrots, marinated coleslaw, and German potato salad. An extensive children's menu is also available.

Desserts are homemade and include pies, pecan rum balls, and walnut, apple, and cinnamon pastries. The unusual lemon lace dessert is lemon sauce layered with French vanilla ice cream and served on a cookie-crumb crust.

A free tour guide service for groups visiting the Amana Colonies is offered, and dinner and theater packages are available with the Old Creamery Theatre Company.

■ Menu Sample

Appetizers: pickled ham, barbecue chicken wings, and barbecue baby back rib sampler.

Family-style dining: all dinners include a cup of soup and refillable bowls of salads, mashed or fried potatoes, brown gravy, garden vegetable, sauerkraut, and warm baked breads.

Dinner items: prime rib, ribeye steak, beef tenderloin, top sirloin, barbecue baby back ribs, apricot chicken breast, *Sauerbraten* (marinated beef), *Wiener Schnitzel* (breaded veal cutlet), *Jäger Schnitzel* (here meaning baby beef cutlet), *Kassler Rippchen* (smoked pork chops), *Rouladen* (braised beef rolls), Swiss steak, hickory-smoked ham steak, bratwurst, fried chicken, jumbo shrimp, scallops, and whitefish.

Lunch: platters of smaller-portion dinner items with soup, salad, and warm bread and butter; sandwiches including reuben, French dip, burgers, ham and cheese, and turkey; or five different salads.

Children's menu: fried chicken, hickory-smoked ham, whitefish, bratwurst, shrimp, burgers, grilled cheese, hot dogs, schnitzel sandwich, soup, cottage cheese, applesauce, and a root beer float.

Sunday brunch: 25 hot and cold entrees and dessert table.

Desserts: homemade pies such as coconut or almond cream and rhubarb crumb; lemon-lace dessert; *Birne Helene* (pear halves, vanilla ice cream, and chocolate sauce); chocolate fudge; pecan rum balls; cheesecake; *Apfelstrudel* (apple strudel); ice cream; sherbet; and chocolate mint or cappuccino ice cream drinks.

Beverages: coffee, espresso, tea, ice tea, milk, chocolate milk, lemonade, bottled water, soft drinks, and apple, tomato, orange, and cranberry juice.

Alcoholic beverages: local and house wines; Glen Ellen and Chateau St. Michelle Chardonnay, Beringer and Sutter Home White Zinfindel, Beringer Gamay Beaujolais, Stone Creek Merlot, and Robert Mondavi and Beringer Cabernet Sauvignon; domestic and imported beers; and mixed drinks and ice cream drinks from the full-service bar.

■ **Brick Haus Restaurant**   [53]

■ QUICK FACTS
Telephone: 319-622-3278/800-622-3471
Hours: open daily, breakfast 7:30 am–10:30 am, lunch 11:00 am–4:00 pm, dinner 11:00 am–8:00 pm
Capacity: 300
Groups: yes
Parking: sizable lot on site of an 1855 granary
Handicap accessible: yes
Smoking: not permitted
Price range: all-you-can-eat breakfast $6.35, lunch $6.25–$6.95, dinner $9.95–$14.75
Payment methods: cash, check, American Express, MasterCard, Visa
Family-style dining: yes
Children's menu: same items for reduced price
Customer favorites: breakfast, German dinner items
Building: constructed 1982 as a restaurant
Restaurant opened: 1982
Hosts: Walt and Florence Schuerer and their daughter and son-in-law, Madeline Schuerer Schulte and Keith "Skeeter" Schulte

At Walt Schuerer's Brick Haus Restaurant, free pie comes with every dinner meal. (Photo by author.)

Dining at the Brick Haus Restaurant is a mixture of good food, lively atmosphere, and engaging conversation. The Schuerer family, which operates the restaurant, has been in the food service business for over 50 years. Walt's grandfather, father, and uncles worked in the village meat shop. His mother and grandmother worked in the communal kitchen houses. Florence's family worked in the communal bakeries.

When Walt returned from the Army in 1946, he went to work operating the Colony Inn Restaurant, which is located across the street. In 1982, his family built the Brick Haus Restaurant and began operations with their daughter Madeline and her husband Keith. They later moved their entire operation to the Brick Haus. Walt's brother Harold operates the Amana Barn Restaurant, and his brother George runs the Grape Vine Winery and Gift Shop.

The Brick Haus is a popular early morning spot, and the large parking lot fills up fast. The all-you-can-eat breakfast is served family style, and the offerings seem endless. The restaurant makes its own corncob syrup, which is offered along with regular maple syrup.

Florence and Walt are early risers, starting off each morning by baking between 75 and 125 pies, which are in the oven by 7:00 am. They offer a free slice of pie or other dessert with every menu entree.

Popular dinner items include many German specialties, such as *Wiener Schnitzel* (breaded veal cutlet) and *Kassler Rippchen* (smoked pork chop), and the seafood items. Pies are also a big hit at the Brick Haus. In addition to the red raspberry and chocolate cream pies, the Brick Haus also makes interesting and popular versions of peanut butter pie and a secret recipe German fruit pie.

Guests at the Brick Haus will find an appreciation for the history of the Amana Colonies and the Schuerers' love of Iowa and the outdoors. Photographs of early Colony activities cover the walls in the dining room areas. The Schuerers, who raise hunting dogs such as German short-haired pointers and Brittanys, also have a series of photographs of their dogs in the restaurant.

Two dining levels are available at the Brick Haus. The bustling main dining areas usually fill up, and overflow guests are accommodated in the lower level. Both levels are carpeted and have rest rooms. The Brick Haus also has an outdoor seating area with benches, tables, and umbrellas. German music is played on a stereo system and sets the tone for the German-style food and hospitality.

Customers are treated like guests in the home, greeted at the door, seated, and pampered by the staff, Walt, and his family. Walt enjoys conversation, and he has a considerable knowledge of early Amana activities.

The Brick Haus offers a free tour service for groups visiting the Colonies and provides dinner and theater packages with the Old Creamery Theatre Company. A gift area is located at the register and offers books, postcards, Amana hats, and food items such as sauerkraut, breads, jams, jellies, and candy.

■ MENU SAMPLE

Breakfast: a la carte items or the all-you-can-eat breakfast, which is served family style and includes chilled orange juice, fruit, fried eggs, fried potatoes, Amana bacon, Amana sausage, pancake with syrup, homemade preserves, toast, and beverage.

Lunch: sandwich platters, which include cheeseburger, pork tenderloin, bratwurst, reuben, turkey, ham, beef, and grilled chicken breast and are served with salad and fries; or plate lunches, which are lighter portions of the dinner menu items.

Family-style dinners include: refillable bowls of cottage cheese, pickled ham, sauerkraut salad, lettuce salad, fruit salad, fried or mashed potatoes, gravy, sauerkraut, two vegetables, such as corn and beans, bread and butter, beverage, and a free dessert.

Dinner items: roast sirloin of beef, Swiss steak, bratwurst (Amana pork sausage), *Wiener Schnitzel* (breaded veal cutlet), sirloin steak, T-bone steak, Amana ham, chicken, boneless chicken breast, lemon herb turkey breast, *Kassler Rippchen* (smoked pork chops), shrimp, scallops, walleye pike fillet, and, on Fridays, pond-raised catfish.

Desserts: free with all entrees; include homemade pies such as chocolate, coconut, or banana cream, peanut butter, apple, red raspberry, cherry, peach, apricot, blueberry, rhubarb, and German fruit pie; strawberry cheesecake, strawberry shortcake; ice cream; sherbet; and sundaes.

Beverages: coffee, tea, iced tea, milk, chocolate milk, hot chocolate, soda, lemonade, and juices.

Alcoholic beverages: local wines and beer choices such as Michelob, Heineken, Löwenbräu, St. Pauli Girl, and Dortmunder, with beer available in fishbowl glasses.

■ Colony Inn Restaurant [59]

■ QUICK FACTS
Telephone: 319-622-6270/800-227-3471
Hours: breakfast 7:00 am–11:00 am daily; lunch Mon–Sat 11:00 am–2:30 pm, Oct–Apr, and 11:00 am–4:00 pm, May–Sept; dinner everyday 4:30 pm–8:00 pm, Sun 11:00 am–7:30 pm
Capacity: 225
Groups: yes
Parking: on street in front, extensive lot in rear, RV parking with hook-ups available
Handicap accessible: yes, accessible stairway on West end of building
Smoking: in designated area only
Price range: breakfast $6.25, lunch $5.50–$7.50, dinner $10–$12, children $2–$6
Payment methods: cash, check, American Express, Discover, Master-Card, Visa
Family-style dining: yes
Children's menu: main menu at reduced price
Customer favorites: Swiss steak, *Kassler Rippchen* (smoked pork chop), rhubarb pie
Building: constructed 1860 as a hotel, 1864 addition
Restaurant opened: 1935
Host: Jim Roemig

The Colony Inn first opened in 1935 and served dinner for 50 cents. (Photo by author.)

The Colony Inn was the first restaurant to open in Amana and began the tradition of family-style dining in the area restaurants. The restaurant had its origins as the Amana Hotel, built of wood in 1860 to accommodate travelers and guests. In 1883, the Chicago, Milwaukee, St. Paul, and Pacific Railroad began servicing Amana, and a brick addition was constructed.

After the Great Change in 1932, Jim's father, Jake Roemig, was in charge of selling the hotels in Homestead, Amana, and South Amana. Jake sold the Amana Hotel but bought it back three years later and opened a restaurant and a 15-room hotel. Jake served up family-style meals for a mere 50 cents. The concept was a big hit, and people came from miles around for the hearty food. This manner of service helped establish both Amana's reputation for abundant food and the tradition of family-style dining.

Later, another addition was added to make the restaurant larger. Jim remembers knocking out one of the walls to make the addition when he was a kid. It was rough work. "It didn't help matters that the early Amana builders had done such a good job," Jim quips.

Today, the Inn offers traditional German food and several popular American dishes. One popular item is Swiss steak . The steak is served in its own gravy with traditional family-style side dishes in refillable bowls. The *Kassler Rippchen* (smoked pork chop) is also popular, as is the hearty wurst platter, which offers bratwurst, seasoned bratwurst, and cheddar cheese bratwurst. All entrees come with a free dessert. The Inn makes 40 pies each weekday and 80 pies on weekend days, and rhubarb pie is the overwhelming favorite.

The interior is representative of Amana tradition. The plain rooms have wooden floors, exposed beams, and wooden tables and booths set with tablecloths. Country decorations hang throughout the restaurant. There are four dining rooms and a smaller eating area by the entryway with several booths and tables. The entryway also has a gift area featuring books, shirts, and food items such as bread, jams and jellies, and Amana

Millstream beer. The Inn also has a landscaped green space for outdoor gatherings.

The restaurant offers getaway packages with Die Heimat Country Inn, Rose's Place Bed and Breakfast, Noé House Inn, and Rawson's Bed and Breakfast. These include one night's accommodation at one of the participating bed and breakfast inns and dinner and breakfast at the Colony Inn.

■ MENU SAMPLE

Breakfast: family style with orange juice, beverage, fruit, pancake and syrup, toasted English muffins, homemade jam, fried eggs, Amana sausage, bacon, and fried potatoes.

Lunch: smaller portions of many dinner items; sandwich platters, which include Swiss steak, roast beef, ham, *Wiener Schnitzel* (breaded veal cutlet), Amana bratwurst, Amana ham, chicken filet, pork tenderloin, reuben, and breaded cod, all served with salad and fries.

Family-style dining: refillable bowls of cottage cheese, green salad, a special salad, mashed or fried potatoes, gravy, German-style sauerkraut, vegetable, and bread and butter.

Dinner: bratwurst platters with smoked, mildly seasoned, and cheddar bratwurst; Amana pork sausage; Amana smoked ham steak; Swiss steak; *Kassler Rippchen* (smoked pork chops); *Sauerbraten* (marinated beef); *Wiener Schnitzel* (breaded veal cutlet); *Jäger Schnitzel* (here meaning pork cutlet); chicken schnitzel; homemade *Spätzle* (German egg noodles); fried chicken; roast beef; fried shrimp; strip steaks; beef tenderloin; orange roughy; catfish; and breaded cod.

Desserts: free with the meal; include pies such as rhubarb, chocolate or coconut cream, and strawberry; strawberry shortcake; strawberry or chocolate sundaes; ice cream; and sherbet.

Beverages: coffee, tea, iced tea, milk, lemonade, soft drinks, Millstream Root Beer, and root beer floats.

Alcoholic beverages: house wines, local wines, Ernest and Julio Gallo wines, sparkling wines, wine coolers, Millstream beers, Heineken, domestic beers, and fishbowl glasses of beer.

Amana

■ Ox Yoke Inn [37]

■ QUICK FACTS
Telephone: 319-622-3441/800-233-3441
Fax: 319-622-6076
Hours: lunch Mon–Sat 11:00 am–4:00 pm; dinner Mon–Sat 4:30 pm–8:00 pm, Sun 12:00 pm–7:00 pm; Sunday brunch 9:00 am–12:00 pm; closed Mon, Nov-Dec, and Mon-Thu, Jan-Feb
Capacity: seats 240 in four dining rooms
Groups: yes
Parking: extensive parking available in rear, bus parking available.
Handicap accessible: yes
Smoking: permitted on second floor, in lobby, and in two lounges
Price range: lunch $6–$9, dinner $8–$17, children $2.50-$6, desserts $2
Payment methods: cash, check, American Express, Diner's Club, Discover, MasterCard, Visa
Family-style dining: yes
Children's menu: yes
Customer favorites: *Wiener Schnitzel* (breaded veal cutlet), fried chicken, rhubarb custard pie with streusel topping

Authentic German food, like **Wiener Schnitzel,** *is available at the Ox Yoke Inn, featured in* **Bon Appétit** *magazine. (Photo by author.)*

Building: constructed 1856 as a communal kitchen house, 1870 wood frame addition
Restaurant opened: 1940, 1950 in present location
Hosts: Bill, Jr., and Karen Lichsenring

The Ox Yoke Inn began serving meals in 1940 for 65 cents. Since then, it has become a favorite spot for visitors and has achieved widespread recognition. The building was constructed in 1856 as a communal kitchen. It was used as a residence after the Great Change in 1932, until Bill and Lina Lichsenring moved their restaurant business to the location in 1950. They had originally opened the restaurant in an old communal kitchen house, which is now the Ronneburg Restaurant.

The Lichsenrings have a strong attachment to the building. When it was a communal kitchen house, it was the Lichsenring kitchen, where Bill's family lived and his mother operated the kitchen. Bill was born in what is now the Amana Room, and his future wife, Lina, worked in the communal kitchen.

Today, Bill Lichsenring, Jr., and his wife, Karen, operate the restaurant. Bill is very involved in the Amana business community and is on the board of directors of the National Restaurant Association. Bill's sister, Kathie Lichsenring Kelly, also works at the restaurant.

The main level consists of a lounge, gift shop, and four dining rooms: the Lily Lake Room, the Amana Room, the Blue Room, and the Woodshed. The Woodshed dining room was an actual woodshed at one time and features Bill and Lina's antique collection. Downstairs consists of a banquet room and the *Bierstube* (beer room) lounge, which Bill, Sr., and friends hand-dug in 1963 when Iowa law began allowing liquor-by-the-drink sales in establishments. The second floor features an antique tool museum and the Ox Yoke's famous stuffed black bear.

One of the specialties of the Inn is *Wiener Schnitzel* or veal. The Ox Yoke uses veal cutlets from Provimi of Wisconsin. To prepare it, the veal is dusted with cracker meal and quickly sautéed in butter. The dish is served with *Spätzle* (German egg noodles) with buttered bread crumbs.

The Inn uses soy oil, Amana ham, pork sausage, beef, fresh baked breads, and homemade pies prepared by workers arriving at 5:00 am. The Ox Yoke offers a number of pies including rhubarb custard with streusel topping.

The Ox Yoke uses one and one-half tons of real potatoes each week. Mashed potatoes are served with lunch and fried potatoes with dinner.

The name, Ox Yoke, was suggested to Bill and Lina by a friend. It refers to the wooden frame by which oxen are joined for working together. The Ox Yoke symbol is a registered trademark, and the restaurant has been featured in *Bon Appétit* magazine and in the "World of Fine Cooking," a national advertising and television promotion by Eagle Foods.

The Ox Yoke offers an Amana Colonies tour guide service, dinner theater packages with the Old Creamery Theatre Company, and overnight packages with the Guest House Motel.

■ Menu Sample

Appetizers: oxen wings, pickled beets, pickled ham, onion rings, garden vegetable beef soup, seafood chowder; chef's salad, seafood pasta salad.

Family-style dining: refillable bowls of cottage cheese, salad, vegetable, hand-peeled mashed or fried potatoes, gravy, sauerkraut, bread and butter, and milk or coffee.

Dinner items: chicken, barbecue ribs, oven-baked steak, Iowa ham, lemon pepper turkey breast, honey apple pork loin, *Wiener Schnitzel* (breaded veal cutlet), *Rhine Schnitzel* (veal with wine and mushroom sauce), *Westphalian Schnitzel* (Westphalian ham and Swiss cheese), *Kassler Rippchen* (smoked pork chops), *Jäger Schnitzel* (here meaning boneless pork loin), chicken schnitzel, *Sauerbraten* (marinated beef), shrimp, whole fresh catfish, codfish, strip steak, sirloin steak, ribeye steak, honey apple pork chop, and swordfish.

Lunch items: include smaller portions of the dinner items as well as platters of bratwurst, pork tenderloin, chicken almond salad, hamburger, charbroiled chicken breast, pepper steak, and hot roast beef and reuben sandwiches.

Sides dishes: potato pancakes, *Spätzle* (German egg noodles), hot German potato salad, red cabbage, and fresh fruit.

Children's menu: hamburger, grilled cheese, and chicken nugget baskets with French fries or fresh fruit; grilled ham and cheese; plate lunches with chicken, roast beef, ham, shrimp or spaghetti; fresh fruit platters; salads; and pizza quesadilla rolls.

Sunday brunch: four entrees, fresh scrambled eggs, potatoes, waffles, salads, fresh pastries, rolls, muffins, juices, coffee, and desserts.

Desserts: homemade pies such as chocolate, coconut, or banana cream, rhubarb custard with streusel topping, rhubarb custard with meringue topping, and pecan; ice cream; strudel; and "death by chocolate," which is chocolate brownies topped with candy bar pieces, coffee liqueur, and whipped cream.

Beverages: milk, hot chocolate, iced tea, coffee, cappuccino, lemonade, orange juice, soft drinks, and sparkling water.

Alcoholic beverages: beers such as Millstream beers, St. Pauli Girl, Becks, DAB, and Berghoff; several local wines; domestic wines such as Columbia Crest Merlot, Stone Creek Cabernet Sauvignon, and R.H. Phillips Sauvignon Blanc; and nonalcoholic beverages including Sharps, O'Douls, Haake Beck, and Clausthaler.

■ The Ronneburg Restaurant [34]

■ QUICK FACTS
Telephone: 319-622-3641
Hours: daily 11:00 am–8:00 pm
Capacity: 130 in three dining rooms and lounge
Groups: yes
Parking: on side and rear of building
Handicap accessible: yes
Smoking: in the lounge dining area
Price range: lunch $2.50–$8.95, dinner $9.95–$19.95
Payment methods: cash, check, American Express, Carte Blanche, Diner's Club, Discover, MasterCard, Visa

Named for a castle in Germany, the Ronneburg Restaurant continues the tradition of German food and hospitality. (Photo by author.)

Family-style dining: yes
Children's menu: main menu at reduced price
Customer favorites: *Sauerbraten* (marinated beef)
Building: constructed 1857 as a communal kitchen house
Restaurant opened: 1950
Hosts: Bill and Elsie Oehler and their son, Don Oehler

The Ronneburg Restaurant is operated by a family with a German tradition reaching back to the early days of the Community of True Inspiration. The Ronneburg is named for a medieval castle in Hesse, Germany. The castle, dating to 1258, served as a sanctuary during the early years of the development of the inspirationist movement. The Ronneburg was one of the handful of estates which offered shelter and freedom of religion to many Germans who sought an alternative to the state-sponsored religion.

Elsie Oehler, one of the owners of the restaurant, is a descendent of a family that lived in the castle. Her grandmother was a kitchen boss in the restaurant building, and Elsie was born in the building. In 1974, Elsie made the first of several trips to the German homeland of her ancestors. "It was very moving to walk in the footsteps of our forebearers," Elsie said. When her son Don saw his mother's pictures of the German countryside he asked his mother, "What is an Amana barn doing there?" Don says Amana resembles the German countryside, so it is no surprise that Amana looked like home to the scouting party that secured the land for the new Colony in 1855.

Today, the Ronneburg Restaurant continues the tradition of hearty German food in a festive environment. One of the more popular items on the menu is the *Sauerbraten*. It is top round roast marinated for several days in spices and local wine and then roasted and covered in its own dark gravy. The dish is served with potato dumplings and side dishes. Elsie says several German tourists have commented that the Ronneburg *Sauerbraten* is superior to what is available in the homeland. In the wintertime, *Rouladen* (braised stuffed beef rolls) is served. Visitors may also get a surprise with rabbit, turtle, walleye, and Friday catfish specials.

Formerly a communal kitchen house, the restaurant still has the original wood floors and exposed beams commonly found in the villages as evidence of the building style of the early Colonists. Two of the restaurant's three dining rooms are simple, Amana-style rooms with wooden floors and exposed beams. The third is a combination lounge/dining area with a full-service bar and a number of tables for dining in a smoking environment.

Adjacent to the Ronneburg is Colony Gardens. It offers a large selection of fine gifts and Christmas items.

■ Menu Sample

Family-style dining: includes refillable bowls of salads, cottage cheese, vegetable, mashed or fried potatoes, gravy, sauerkraut, and bread and butter.

Dinner items: *Sauerbraten* (marinated beef), *Wiener Schnitzel* (breaded veal cutlet), sliced Amana ham, Amana pork sausage, pork chops, ribeye steak, T-bone steak, porterhouse steak, fried chicken, and a number of seafood items including walleye, catfish, pike, shrimp, jumbo shrimp, and tilapia (a locally raised white fish).

Lunch and sandwiches: bratwurst, knockwurst, breaded pork tenderloin, breaded chicken, shrimp baskets, reuben, sirloin burgers, hot roast beef with fried potatoes and gravy, grilled chicken salad, and Bavarian salad.

Desserts: homemade pies including rhubarb custard, peach pecan, Dutch apple, coconut or banana cream, and fresh strawberry; chocolate sauerkraut cake with rose water icing; black forest brownie with vanilla ice cream and cherry sauce; strawberry shortcake; cheesecake; hazelnut sundae; and ice cream.

Beverages: coffee, tea, iced tea, soft drinks, and milk.

Alcoholic beverages: coffee drinks, imported brandy, domestic beers, Millstream beers, Heineken, and locally produced wines.

Lodging Facilities

■ Amana Colonies RV Park [6]

■ Quick Facts
Telephone: 319-622-7616
Fax: 319-622-6137
Open for use: Apr 15–Nov 1
Capacity: 500 RVs, plus 100 temporary sites for major conventions
Sites: 125 level graveled sites with electric and water hook-ups
Total acres: 60
Check-in: anytime
Check-out: 1:00 pm
Rates: campers and RVs $12 per day, tents $8 per day
Payment methods: cash, check, Discover, MasterCard, Visa
Amenities: showers and restrooms, coin laundry, general store, dump site
Convention accommodations: one 12,000-square-foot building with heating and air-conditioning, one 5,600-square-foot building

The Amana Colonies RV Park can accommodate 500 campers and large conventions. (Photo courtesy of Amana Colonies RV Park.)

Pets: on leash only
Prohibited: campfires, motorbikes, vehicle washing
Park opened: 1991
Owner: Amana Society
Manager: Rhett Simmons

The Amana Colonies RV Park opened for visitors in 1991 and has grown into a sizable facility, playing host to a number of large conventions. Growing yearly, the Park can handle major conventions and over 500 RVs. The 12,000-square-foot convention facility can accommodate 1,200 people for banquets and dinners in its heated and air-conditioned building.

For standard RV traffic, the Park has several amenities including restrooms, showers, a coin-operated laundry, a small playground area for children, a general store, and dump sites.

At the general store, RV supplies include drain hoses, water hoses, and electric plugs. Groceries include hamburger, bratwurst, bacon, and the charcoal to grill them with. Also available are soup, milk, juice, beer, and various sundries such as shampoo, soap, and over-the-counter medical supplies.

The Park also offers security lighting and fenced grounds.

■ Guest House Motel [52]

■ QUICK FACTS
Telephone: 319-622-3599
Number of rooms: 12 in the old building, 26 in the modern unit
Rate range: $36–$52
Payment methods: cash, check, American Express, Discover, MasterCard, Visa
Reservations: recommended
Check-in: 2:00 pm, will hold until 4:00 pm without credit card
Check-out: 11:00 am
Private baths: yes
Amenities: air-conditioning, color television with cable and HBO, private phones, two tanning rooms
Breakfast: no
Parking: space between two buildings

The 1860 sandstone Guest House Motel also has a modern motel next door. (Photo by author.)

Handicap accessible: yes, three rooms are handicap accessible
Smoking: in smoking rooms
Children: yes
Pets: no
Building: constructed as a communal kitchen house building in 1860, with the modern unit built in 1984 as a motel
Motel opened: both buildings opened in 1984
Owner: Les Roemig

The Guest House Motel has two separate buildings a few yards apart. The Guest House offers visitors rooms in either an old communal kitchen house or a modern motel unit. In the early 1980s, motel owner Les Roemig was on a fruit buying trip for a winery when he saw a plan for a modular motel. Les liked the plan and decided to build a modular motel building next to the site of the communal kitchen house. He built the new motel unit in 1984, remodeled the communal kitchen house, and opened them both for business.

The original building was constructed in 1860 and was converted to a single-family home after the Great Change in 1932. The sandstone walls from the kitchen remain in many of the rooms. There are nine single- and three double-bed rooms. All of the rooms are spacious, some with sloping ceilings and four-poster beds made in the Amana Furniture Shop. Several rooms feature European-style bathrooms with sinks in the bedroom area.

The new 26-unit motel features 23 rooms with double beds and three rooms with twin beds. All of the rooms are carpeted. The building has two tanning rooms available for guests and a front desk which provides 24-hour assistance.

The rooms in both buildings are air-conditioned and have color television with cable and HBO, private telephones, and full private bathrooms. The rooms in the old communal kitchen house are furnished with older pieces to accent the historic home. The new unit has modern motel furnishings.

The Guest House Motel offers packages in conjunction with the Ox Yoke Inn which feature overnight accommodations at the Guest House with dinner and lunch or brunch at the Ox Yoke Inn.

■ Noé House Inn [39]

■ QUICK FACTS
Telephone: 319-622-6350
Number of rooms: four
Rate range: $55–$75
Payment methods: cash, check, American Express, Discover, Master-Card, Visa
Reservations: recommended
Check-in: 1:00 pm–3:00 pm
Check-out: 11:00 am
Private baths: yes
Amenities: air-conditioning, cable television, handmade quilts
Breakfast: continental breakfast on weekend only
Parking: in rear
Handicap accessible: one lower level room is accessible
Smoking: no
Children: 10 and older
Pets: no

A king-size four-poster canopy bed at the Noé House Inn. (Photo by author.)

Building: constructed 1856 as a communal kitchen house and residence with an addition in 1881
Inn opened: 1992
Hosts: owners not in residence

Located on the main street of Amana, the Noé House Inn is one of only two lodging facilities in the village of Amana. Owner Barbara Brown and her family converted this private residence to a four-bedroom inn in 1992. The Inn has wooden floors with area rugs and old-style locks made by the early Colonists.

Two bedrooms, the Sunday Room and the Hidden Room, are on the ground level. The Sunday Room is handicap accessible and was once a parlor room. It features a king-size, four-poster canopied bed and a bureau. Light colors, a leaf border, and a hand-stenciled rose-and-flower pattern decorate the walls. The private full bathroom has a tub/shower unit. The Hidden Room is similar and features a full-size bed, closet space, and a bathroom with a shower. Both rooms have wooden floors with rugs.

Upstairs consists of the Green Room and the Blue Room. The Green Room features a queen-size bed on a four-poster frame, a chair and ottoman, and a bureau. The walls are light green with a rose border. The connecting bathroom has a shower unit, and the sink is in the bedroom, just outside the bathroom door. The roomy Blue Room has two full-size beds on walnut frames, a chair and ottoman, a chest, and a bureau. The room is decorated in dark blue with light walls and a blue floral pattern. Various country prints are found in the room. The full bathroom is two doors down the hall.

Breakfast is available on the weekend and includes fruit soup, pastries, cereal, juice, and coffee. Barb says her weekday guests, many of whom include professionals and retired couples, tend to be early risers and enjoy breakfast at one of the several area restaurants.

Breakfast is served in a dining area at a large table with highback chairs. Also available is an adjacent kitchen with a refrigerator and coffeemaker. The connecting parlor room offers a spacious, relaxing area with a number of chairs, rockers, benches, and coffee tables. An authentic Amana rug is on the floor.

Originally a communal kitchen house, the home was built in 1856 for Wilhelm Noé (1804–1882), a map maker, who was one of the three men who traveled to America with Colony leader Christian Metz in 1842 to search for a new home for the Inspirationists. The Noé family lived in the house for 135 years.

Located adjacent to the Noé House Inn are three popular businesses run by Barbara: the Christmas Room, the Red Geranium, and the Gingerbread House.

Shops and Tourist Attractions

■ Amana Church Society

Telephone: 319-622-6155
Sunday service: held in Middle Amana, German service 8:30 am,
English service 10:00 am

The large church in Amana is still utilized for various services and special occasions. However, regular Sunday services are conducted at the Middle Amana Church, with a German service at 8:30 am and an English service at 10:00 am. See the listing under Middle Amana Church in Middle Amana for more information about services.

The church building was built in 1864. The basement was used as a wine and potato cellar. The Amana Welfare Association, formed after the Great Change in 1932 to provide social activities for the Colonists, got its start in the cellar in 1933. The Welfare Association later moved its headquarters to the building which now houses Smokehouse Square Antiques.

■ Amana Colonies Convention and [3] Visitors Bureau (ACCVB)

Telephone: 319-622-7622/800-245-5465
Hours: Mon–Fri 8:00 am–4:30 pm

Physically connected to the Amana Colonies Visitors Center, the ACCVB works to accommodate visitors and convention activities for the Amana Colonies. The Bureau helps arrange outdoor events or indoor corporate meetings and seminars using various multipurpose facilities including a 300-seat theater, private meeting rooms, 60 acres of developed exhibit sites, two large conference buildings, and a recreational vehicle park. Bureau personnel staff the Amana Colonies Visitors Center.

■ Amana Colonies Visitors Center [2]

Telephone: 800-245-5465
Hours: Mon–Fri 9:00 am–5:00 pm; also open during Old Creamery Theatre performances

This is a one-stop tourist center with information on village attractions, lodging reservation access, theater ticket purchases, a book and gift shop, and a snack bar. The Visitors Center is one of the State of Iowa's Welcome Centers, designed to provide information and direction to visitors.

■ Amana Farmer's Market [48]

Telephone: none
Hours: open seasonally

Located behind Tiny Tim's Colony Christmas and across from the Broom and Basket Shop, the Farmer's Market offers local produce on a very limited seasonal basis.

■ Amana Furniture Shop [61]

Telephone: 319-622-3291/800-247-5088
Hours: Mon–Sat 9:00 am–6:00 pm, Sun 12:00 pm–5:00 pm

The Furniture Shop building was built in 1861 as a calico mill but was later converted to a cabinet shop. It now houses a full line of solid oak, cherry, and walnut items. Visitors can tour the workshop and learn about early furniture making in the Colonies. A short videotape presentation gives details on furniture making.

Shoppers can purchase bedroom, living room, dining room, and office pieces as well as a large selection of floor, mantle, and wall clocks, all made in the German tradition. The shop will custom-make any item and also offers polishes and stains.

The Amana Furniture Shop offers handcrafted pieces with a 100-year guarantee. (Photo by author.)

The Furniture Shop takes great care in creating high-quality, durable items. Their time-honored processes include the use of mortise and tenon joints rather than dowel joints, dovetail joints for drawers, back rail and center drawer glides, solid wood splines on all mitered corners, and several coats of handrubbed varnish to create these masterpieces. Each piece is created by a single craftsperson and is offered with a 100-year guarantee.

■ Amana General Store [25]

Telephone: 319-622-7650
Hours: Mon–Sat 8:30 am–6:00 pm, Sun 11:00 am–5:00 pm

Built in 1856 as a general store and residence, this building also housed the Amana Society business office from 1932 to 1973. For a time, a beer room was located in the rear of the building.

This 1856 general store now offers gifts, crafts, food, and Amana appliances. (Photo by author.)

The General Store now offers a wide selection of gift items, with the focus on Amana, and a showroom of Amana appliances including refrigerators, washers, dryers, and microwave ovens. Other items include crafts, books, quilts, baskets, collectibles, shirts, souvenirs, tablecloths, food items, candy, toys, and cards. The downstairs level has a selection of steins and local wines.

■ Amana Handimart [30]

Telephone: 319-622-3270
Hours: daily 6:00 am–11:00 pm, Fri until 1:00 am

The only stop for fuel in the Amana Colonies is the Amana Handimart, a convenience store with all the typical food and sundry items. Also located inside the store is Nordy's Subs &

Salads, which prepares freshly made deli items. This building originally was built in 1932 as a gas station and sandwich shop. An ATM cash machine is located here.

■ Amana Heritage Society

Telephone: 319-622-3567 for information

The Amana Heritage Society was created in 1968 to assist in the preservation of the cultural heritage of the Colonies. The Society identifies, collects, preserves, and displays artifacts, books, photographs, and documents of Amana history. The Society operates four museums in the Colonies: the Museum of Amana History in Amana, the Amana Community Church in Homestead, the Communal Agriculture Museum in South Amana, and the Communal Kitchen and Coopershop Museum in Middle Amana. The Heritage Society offers membership to those interested in assisting with these endeavors.

The Society also offers guided walking tours in Amana as part of the tour of the Museum of Amana History. Walking tours last around an hour. A guide points out significant buildings, gives a brief history of the Colonies, and answers questions. Walking tours are Monday–Saturday at 11:30 am and 2:30 pm and Sunday at 2:30 pm. They depart from the Museum of Amana History.

■ Amana Meat Shop and Smokehouse   [10]

Telephone: 319-622-7580/800-373-6328
Fax: 800-373-3710
Hours: Mon–Sat 8:30 am–5:00 pm, Sun and holidays
    11:00 am–4:00 pm

This old smokehouse was built in 1856 and provided a location for butchering and curing meats for the village of Amana. In the

Meats hung in the tower of the Amana Meat Shop and Smokehouse are hickory smoked. (Photo by author.)

communal days, each village had its own meat shop and smokehouse where meats were processed for use in the communal kitchens. The only other remaining, operating meat shop is located in Homestead.

Today visitors can purchase a variety of Amana meats including steaks, roasts, pork chops, sausage, bratwurst, ham, and bacon. Other food items include cheese, bread, noodles, jellies, syrups, and horseradish sauce. Gift items such as mugs, books, and Amana blankets are also available. At the store, visitors can sample several items and pick up a mail-order catalog if they wish to place telephone orders.

■ Amana Stone Hearth Bakery [44]

Telephone: 319-622-7640
Hours: Mon–Sat 8:00 am–5:00 pm, Sun 9:00 am–4:00 pm

In the communal days, all the villages had bakeries which provided baked items for the communal kitchen. Today, the Amana Stone Hearth Bakery provides plenty of baked goods as well as other food products. Shoppers can purchase items to go.

Sandwiches made from local bread and meats, homemade breads, pastries, strudel, turnovers, cookies, noodles, ice cream, coffee, desserts, candy, and various drinks are available. The bakery has ample seating in an upstairs loft as well as on a small front porch bench where one can eat while watching the traffic pass.

The building was constructed in 1856 as a communal residence, although the front porch was added at a later time.

■ Amana Woolen Mill [63]

Telephone: 319-622-3432/800-222-6430
Hours: Mon–Sat 8:00 am–6:00 pm, Sun 11:00 am-5:00 pm

The Amana Woolen Mill has operated since 1855 and was an integral part of Amana's economy during the communal days. The buildings were constructed over a period of time from 1854 to 1860. The third-story frame portion of the building burned in a devastating explosion and fire in 1923 which destroyed 13 buildings. The frame portion was not rebuilt.

Today shoppers can purchase coats, jackets, ponchos, sport coats, sweaters, robes, neckties, pillows, throw rugs, and popular Amana blankets at the Woolen Mill. Fabric and wool pelts are available, as are place settings, napkins, wine bottle covers, yarn "Mill Dolls," stuffed animals, Christmas tree skirts, and yarn angels.

Amana wool blankets were sold to the U.S. Army and, during World War II, as well as to the Russian Army. They were also used in the 1995 Civil War television movie "Andersonville."

The Amana Mill is the only operating woolen mill in Iowa. It produces Amana blankets on two modern, computerized looms and one 1940s-vintage loom (also used for demonstrations). Self-guided tours allow visitors to walk through the mill and watch the warping and weaving operation. Outside, you can find the millrace, or canal, which was built by the Colonists to power the woolen mill and other mill operations. There is a woolen mill outlet at the Little Amana complex on Interstate 80.

■ Antique Tower Haus [17]

Telephone: 319-622-3888
Hours: Mon–Fri 9:00 am–5:00 pm, Sat 10:00 am–5:00 pm, Sun 12:00 pm–5:00 pm

This gift shop offers collectibles and antiques including Boyd's Bears, Snowbabies, Precious Moments, Cherished Teddies, stoneware, tins, miniatures, and chimes.

The building was built around 1885 and was used as a pharmacy annex. The tower was used to dry hog bellies. From the hog's belly, the pharmacist would scrape away a substance called pepsin, which was a product used to alleviate an upset stomach.

■ Antiques and Things [8]

Telephone: 319-622-6461
Hours: Mon–Sat 9:00 am–5:00 pm

This spacious antique shop, next door to the Colony Cone, features collectibles, doll houses, crafts, and a variety of typical antique items including furniture, crocks, and wall hangings. Visitors will also find a variety of kitchen tools and sleigh bells.

The building was a communal residential home built in 1855. The windows have nine-over-six-pane glass. This window structure and design was common in the New England states during the mid-1850s and is found in buildings throughout the Amanas.

■ Broom and Basket Shop [50]

Telephone: 319-622-3311
Hours: Mon–Sat 9:00 am–5:00 pm, Sun 12:00 pm–5:00 pm

This shop has a large variety of baskets and dozens of different brooms, each type designed for a different purpose. Also available are candle holders, foot stools, rolling pins, cradles, quilt holders, rugs, recipe boxes, picture frames, stains, and oils. This store is connected with the broom and basket shops and the Schanz Furniture stores in South and West Amana. Check with the clerk for demonstration times.

This building was used as a residence and watchtower in communal days. The watchman had a good view of the mills and the barns. The exact date it was built is unclear, and the tower has since been removed.

■ Carole's Giftshop [29]

Telephone: 319-622-3570
Hours: Daily 9:00 am–6:00 pm

Carole's offers a wide array of used and antique items in the upper level. The ground level features Iowa cookbooks, old books, honey, crafts, potpourri, antiques, trademarked Hog Iowa T-shirts, embossing stamps, sports cards, dolls, Amish dolls, Amish prints, lamp shades, candles, quilt racks, old instruments, and afghans. Handcrafted stoneware and jewelry from Blackbird Pottery, a local artist's company, is also available. Carole's is believed to have been an 1893 communal residence.

■ The Christmas Room [42]

Telephone: 319-622-3692
Hours: Mon–Thu 9:00 am–5:30 pm, Fri–Sat 9:00 am–6:00 pm,
 Sun 10:00 am–5:00 pm

This old double garage now houses an array of Christmas-related items, including over 1,500 styles of ornaments as well as nutcrackers, smokers, collectible Santas, Byer's Choice Carolers, Department 56 lighted villages, Old World glass ornaments, Fontanini heirloom nativities, and locally made wreaths. The Christmas Room is part of Noé House, an old communal kitchen and residence built in 1856. This was the first Christmas shop in the villages.

■ Clothes Encounter [36]

Telephone: 319-622-3648
Hours: Mon–Sat 9:00 am–6:00 pm, Sun 11:00 am–5:00 pm

This boutique features fine women's clothing, sweaters, and jewelry as well as T-shirts, sweatshirts, and novelty sweaters. Some men's and children's clothing is also available. Clothes Encounter is operated by Elsie Oehler and her daughter. Elsie runs the adjacent Ronneburg Restaurant, built in 1857 as a communal kitchen and residence.

■ Colony Candleworks [18]

Telephone: 319-622-3879
Hours: Mon–Sat 9:00 am–5:00 pm, Sat 9:00 am–6:00 pm,
  Sun 11:00 am–5:00 pm

Part of the old pharmacy complex in the village of Amana, today the Colony Candleworks dispenses a large variety of candles, candle-making items, and accessories in a number of scents, shapes, and colors. Visitors can watch handrolled beeswax candles being made throughout the day Monday through Friday. The building was built around 1900 as a dentist's office, which was part of the pharmacy complex located in this area.

■ The Colony Cone   [7]

Telephone: 319-622-3183
Hours: daily 11:00 am–9:00 pm, Mar–Oct

The Colony Cone is an ice cream shop and short-order grill. Ice cream offerings include floats; malts; shakes; vanilla, chocolate, and twist cones; banana splits; parfait; and hot fudge brownies. Flavors run the gamut from marshmallow or pineapple to Oreo cookie or Snickers.

Grilled items include quarter-pound hamburgers, cheeseburgers, bacon cheeseburgers, pizza burgers, tenderloin, fish, Amana bratwurst, chicken strips, steak sandwiches, turkey club, hot dogs, and corn dogs with sides such as French fries, onion rings, crispy curls, and cheeseballs. Soft drinks, lemonade, iced tea, coffee, and milk are available. The Colony Cone can seat about 30 people.

Built as a steamed-powered sawmill in 1858, this structure burned in 1871.

■ Colony Gardens   [35]

Telephone: 319-622-3837
Hours: Mon–Sat 9:00 am–6:00 pm, Sun 10:00 am–5:00 pm

Fine gifts, florals and accessories, collectibles, candles, bath items, Porter music boxes, and Christmas items await the shopper at this former communal kitchen and residence built in 1857. The proprietors also operate Tiny Tim's Colony Christmas. The Ronneburg Restaurant is adjacent to Colony Gardens.

■ Colony Inn Candy Store   [56]

Telephone: 319-622-3722
Hours: Mon–Fri 10:00 am–5:00 pm, Sat 10:00 am–6:00 pm, Sun 11:00 am–6:00 pm

The Colony Inn Candy Store tempts the shopper with a number of choices of homemade fudge such as "pecan heavenly goo," and a well-stocked supply of candy which includes licorice, candy sticks, and bagged chocolates. Also available are ice cream, soft drinks, and gift items such as soda glasses.

■ Colony Visits/Heritage Destinations [5]

Telephone: 319-622-6178/319-622-3532
Fax: 319-622-3958
Hours: Mon–Fri 9:00 am–5:00 pm or, in summer, 9:00 am–9:00 pm; Sat–Sun 10:00 am–6:00 pm

This business offers the following services for group visitors to the Amana Colonies: charter transportation; guided tours; overnight packages which include accommodations, meals, and entertainment; single-day packages with meals; and theater packages. Colony Visits hosts large and small groups, schools, churches, leisure groups, tour groups, meetings, conventions, and reunions.

For individuals and families, the service includes a sight-seeing tour of the villages each Saturday morning. It departs from a location near the Destinations office at the Amana Colonies Convention and Visitors Bureau.

■ Country Connection [51]

Telephone: 319-622-6191
Hours: Mon–Sat 10:00 am–5:00 pm, Sun 12:00 pm–5:00 pm

Country Connection offers a large selection of dried flowers, floral arrangements, and fine gifts. The accent is on country and on homemade crafts. Shoppers will find furniture and accessories, plates, stuffed animals, candles, greeting cards, birdhouses, bath soaps, gourmet items, and a Christmas room with angels, wreaths, and ornaments. Paintings and folk art are also available.

This structure was the residential portion of the 1860 community kitchen which is now The Guest House Motel. The two buildings were separated and the residence moved to its present location.

■ Creative Colony [46]

Telephone: 319-622-3753
Hours: Mon–Sat 9:00 am–6:00 pm, Sun 10:00 am–5:00 pm

Originally built as a residence in 1881, this building now offers handmade gifts by Iowa artists. The vast array of gift items includes Christmas village pieces made of brick, children's trains built with interconnecting letters of the alphabet, wicker items, stained glass, pottery, ceramics, dolls, various animal replicas, rugs, stencils, jewelry, dried floral arrangements, and woodcraft items ranging from magazine racks to toy trucks. The Colony features a Christmas room and gift items with country, Southwestern, Western, and Victorian themes.

■ Der Weinkeller [15]

Telephone: 319-622-3630
Hours: Mon–Sat 9:30 am–5:00 pm, Sun 10:00 am–5:00 pm

A full line of locally produced fruit and table wines are available in this building, which was part of the pharmacy built in 1867. It housed the pharmacy and doctor's office until 1932, when the doctor moved his office to the home across the street, which is now the Museum of Amana History.

Weinkeller refers to a place where wine was stored. Today, wines offered by Der Weinkeller include rhubarb, dandelion, peach, raspberry, cherry, Catawba, Johnannisberg Riesling, and

Chenin Blanc. Several wines have won awards at various wine fairs and competitions; these include the blueberry, cranberry, and plum varieties. Visitors may sample the wines and walk through the cellar.

■ Erenberger Antiques [12]

Telephone: 319-622-3230
Hours: Mon–Sat 11:00 am–5:00 pm, Sun 12:00 pm–5:00 pm

Erenberger's is a traditional antique shop featuring pine and primitives on the original-surface floor of an 1870 communal residential home. Connected to Renate's Antique Gallery, this shop also features stoneware and various accessories. Renate's and Erenberger's compliment one another and offer a large selection of items in their 12 rooms.

■ Fenn Works [64]

Telephone: 319-622-3710/800-227-8966
Hours: daily 10:00 am–5:00 pm

Fenn Works is a glassblowing and woodcraft shop. Visitors can watch the artistry of glassblowing as the furnace temperature reaches 3,500 degrees. Check with the shop for various times.

In addition to glass items such as ornaments and paperweights, Fenn Works offers many handmade wood items, including fretwork (intricate scrolled woodwork), made from nearby Iowa oak, walnut, and cherry woods. Collapsible baskets, clocks, and handpainted seasonal gifts for Christmas, Thanksgiving, Easter, and other occasions are also available. The work is intricate and detailed. For example, 1,200 blade changes were required to produce a wooden replica of the Lord's Prayer which hangs on one wall.

■ Gingerbread House [41]

Telephone: 319-622-6346
Hours: Mon–Thu 9:00 am–5:30 pm, Fri–Sat 9:00 am–6:00 pm, Sun 10:00 am–5:00 pm

Gingerbread House focuses on homespun fabrics, craft patterns, and ceramic buttons. Shoppers will also find decorative birdhouses, quilts, floral arrangements, and many Christmas items. Fine women's clothing is also offered.

■ Grape Vine Winery and Gift Shop [11]

Telephone: 319-622-3698
Hours: daily 10:00 am–4:30 pm

Located adjacent to the Amana Meat Shop and Smokehouse, the Grape Vine offers a wine shop, gift shop, and Kris Kringle's Christmas Store, all in one place. Small Christmas trees, figurines, ornaments, Santas, and sleighs compete with European lace curtains and rhubarb, plum, and raspberry wines. A full-service wine store offers 16 samples to taste or carry out. The gift shop has many items including dolls, antiques, and toys. This old communal residence was built in 1873.

■ Great Midwest Leather [45]

Telephone: 319-622-6069
Hours: Mon–Sat 10:00 am–5:00 pm, Sun 11:00 am–4:30 pm

This shop offers a variety of leather goods, and the proprietor casts molten pewter to create gifts or custom-made items such as belt buckles, medallions, and figurines. Stop in to watch the work or take home one of the beautiful Amana village figurines. Leather belts, bags, jackets, vests, purses, wallets, briefcases, hats, Western hats, and Native American artwork are available, as are moccasins and other Native American wear.

■ Heritage Designs Needlework and Quilting [27]

Telephone: 319-622-3887
Hours: Mon–Sat 10:00 am–5:00 pm, Sun 11:00 am–4:00 pm

An abundant selection of quilting supplies including fabrics, patterns, books, stencils, and related items such as cross stitch, needlepoint, hardanger, doll and craft patterns, and handmade buttons. Fabrics include designs from Hoffman, RJR-Jinny Beyer, Gutcheon, Alexander Henry, Marcus Brothers, and Liberty of London. Classes are offered. The building was a communal residence built in 1870.

■ Heritage Wine and Cheese Haus [33]

Telephone: 319-622-3564
Hours: daily 9:00 am–6:00 pm

This building was a communal residence, tinsmith, and watchmaker's shop. This winery is connected with the Ackerman Winery in South Amana and features both award-winning fruit wines (including elderberry, blackberry, and black raspberry) and dinner wines. The winery has received over 50 awards since 1990 in nation-wide competitions such as the New World International Competition, the Pacific Rim International Wine Competition, the Los Angeles County Fair, the American Wine Society Competition, and the National Wine Competition.

Heritage has a large gift selection. They offer over 50 imported and domestic cheeses; a number of other foods such as jams, jellies, roasted corn, and horseradish; and many other items such as kitchen utensils, rugs, blankets, baskets, doorstops, cast iron toys, and chimes.

■ Kitchen Sink [58]

Telephone: 319-622-3227
Hours: Mon–Sat 9:00 am–6:00 pm, Sun 11:00 am–5:00 pm

Gourmet kitchen wares, kitchen furnishings, and coffee overflow in the Kitchen Sink, an old communal kitchen built in 1872. Shoppers will find Calphalon cookware, knives, mugs, crocks, cookie jars, terra cotta items, Lodge cast iron, baskets, aprons, oven mitts, place mats, napkins, linens, pans, pot racks, cake pans, cookie cutters, coffee, tea, spices, and various gifts.

■ Lehm Books and Gifts [22]

Telephone: 319-622-6447
Hours: Mon–Sat 9:30 am–5:00 pm, Sun 12:00 pm–5:00 pm

This book and gift shop shares the 1857 church building, residence, and one-time shoemaker's shop with Olde World Lace Shoppe. Note the sundial on the south exterior wall, one of only three sundials in the Colonies.

Today shoppers will find a considerable collection of books for children and young adults as well as a selection of current novels, classics, and biographies for older readers. Visitors will also find prints, florals, crafts, angel replicas and angel books, and a wide selection of toy farm equipment and farm equipment books. The store has Christmas and greeting cards, bookends, collector dolls, puppets, various crafts, baskets and other gifts.

■ Lily Lake [1]

Telephone: none
Hours: accessible year-round

Once a marshy area, Lily Lake was created when it was filled with water following the construction of the millrace (canal),

Amana

around 1865. The American lotus, or yellow *Nelumbo*, bursts open every summer around July and covers the pond with bright yellow color for several weeks.

A picnic area with grills, picnic tables, and a small covered shelter with tables is available along the roadside. Migrating birds such as Canada geese, blue herons, and pelicans can be found at the lake.

■ Maddie's/Der Laden Apparel and Gifts [54]

Telephone: 319-622-3811
Hours: Everyday 9:00 am–5:00 pm

Der Laden (the store) features fine apparel and gifts including clothing, jewelry, accessories, and shoes, as well as bath items and Hummels. Crabtree and Evelyn soaps and toiletries, Aromatique decorative fragrances, and Root and Riguad scented candles fill the store. Clothing includes women's sweaters, casual separates, suits, and evening wear. The building was a communal residence and is now operated by Madeline Schuerer Schulte who, with her family, runs the adjacent Brick Haus Restaurant. Madeline also operates the Red Fox Paper Den, which is located next door to Der Laden.

■ Millstream Brewing Company [60]

Telephone: 319-622-3672
Hours: Mon–Sat 9:00 am–6:00 pm, Sun 11:00 am–5:00 pm

One of only a handful of microbreweries in America when it opened in 1985, the Millstream Brewing Company has carved a comfortable niche in the exploding market for microbrewed beer. Millstream offers three beers and a root beer. The beers are Millstream Lager, a well-aged lager with a creamy head; Schild Brau Amber, a European brew in the tradition of the *Oktoberfest*

One of the first microbreweries in America was the Millstream Brewing Company, which makes several award-winning beers. (Photo by author.)

beers of Germany; and Millstream Wheat, blended with wheat and barley and served with either a slice of lemon or raspberry syrup. For several years, the Schild Brau and Wheat beers have won either first or second place awards at the annual Great American Beer Fest in Denver.

Visitors can sample the beers and the root beer in the tasting room or in the restful outdoor beer garden, located near the old Amana millrace, from which Millstream Brewing derives its name. The millrace, or canal, was used to power the woolen mill and other mills once located in this area.

The entire brewing process is completed on site. First, the barley and/or wheat is ground and steeped with water to produce wort, a sweet liquid. Following this process, the wort is boiled with hops, then cooled to combine with yeast for fermenting. The beer is cellared to age and then naturally carbonated through the *krausening* process to arrive at the desired flavor. The microbrewery can produce 620 gallons of beer per day, which is roughly 6,500 bottles. No chemicals, additives, or preservatives are used in the products.

Visitors can take home the beer, root beer, caps, T-shirts, polo shirts, mugs, glasses, and coasters.

■ Museum of Amana History [32]

Telephone: 319-622-3567
Hours: Apr 15–Nov 15, Mon–Sat 10:00 am–5:00 pm, Sun 12:00 pm–5:00 pm. Also open for various events throughout the winter

The Museum of Amana History offers well-developed and displayed presentations on the history of the Amana Colonies. The main building offers exhibits tracing the history of the Community of True Inspiration from its beginnings in Germany through the voyage across the ocean to New York and, finally, to Iowa.

The Museum presents information on nearly all facets of village life. An adjacent washhouse/woodshed features gardening and wine-making tools and displays. A few hundred feet along the narrow sidewalk is the schoolhouse, which offers an audiovisual presentation about the Colonies and displays school artifacts, photographs, and other items from earlier Colony times. In the schoolhouse, an extensive array of reading material on the Colonies is for sale. The schoolhouse also contains the Museum's library and archives.

The main building was built in 1874 as a communal kitchen and residence for Amana's first physician, Dr. Heinrich Fehr. After Fehr died, it became the Trautmann kitchen house until 1918, when Dr. and Mrs. Charles Noé lived in the home and communal kitchen. Noé had his office across the street, in the building that today houses the Village Pastry Shop and Der Weinkeller, until the Great Change of 1932, at which time he moved his office to his home. The Amana Heritage Society secured this building for the Museum in 1967. The schoolhouse was built in 1870

The Museum of Amana History offers a range of historical artifacts, information, and tours. (Photo by author.)

and was used as a school until 1954. It was later used as a post office and Sunday school. The Amana Heritage Society acquired the schoolhouse building in 1976.

Admission is $3 for adults, $1 for children, and free for those under age eight. Group rates are available. Combination tickets for the four Amana Heritage Society museums are also available.

■ Nordy's Subs & Salads   [31]

Telephone: 319-622-3028
Hours: Mon-Sat 6:00 am–9:00 pm, Sun 8:00 am-8:00 pm

Nordy's is located inside the Amana Handimart, a convenience store which is the only stop in the Amana Colonies for fuel. The counter business offers subs, sandwiches, and salads, and also caters deli food items. This building originally was built in 1932 as a gas station and sandwich shop. An ATM cash machine is located here.

■ Oak Ridge Gallery [43]

Telephone: 319-622-6338
Hours: Mon-Sat 9:00 am-6:00 pm, Sun 11:00 am-5:00 pm

This gallery offers limited edition prints, custom framing, plates, carvings, and collectibles with a special emphasis on wildlife, Native American pieces, the Southwest, and rural scenes. The Gallery features the work of Redlin, Liu, Bateman, Peterson, and Doolittle; Linda Bennett's Amish work; and handcarved originals by Barry Stein. The building was a communal residence built in 1881.

■ Old Creamery Theatre Company [4]

Telephone: 319-622-6194/800-352-6262
Fax: 319-622-6187
Hours: Mon–Fri 8:00 am–4:30 pm for tickets or leave message on machine

The Old Creamery Theatre Company offers live theater by a professional company from March through December each year. The company has been performing in Iowa since 1971 and is recognized as the premier theater group in the state.

Old Creamery performs in the theater at the Amana Colonies Convention and Visitors Bureau. Performance information and tickets are available at that location or by phone. The new theater is air-conditioned and handicap accessible. Performance times are generally at 8:00 pm Friday and Saturday and at 3:00 pm on Thursday and Sunday. The ticket price range is approximately $15-$25, and group rates are available. In addition, several area restaurants offer packages for dinner and theater.

■ Old Wine Cellar Winery [21]

Telephone: 319-622-3116
Fax: 319-622-6162
Hours: Mon–Fri 9:00 am–6:00 pm, Sat 9:00 am–7:00 pm, Sun 10:00 am–5:00 pm

Wine, cheese, candy, and gifts are available at the Old Wine Cellar Winery. The Winery offers tastings and has a fine selection of award-winning wines such as their 1995 raspberry, plum, and cranberry wines, all winners at the Indiana State Fair. This building was originally an 1857 communal residence and shoe shop.

■ Olde World Lace Shoppe [23]

Telephone: 319-622-3097
Hours: Mon–Sat 9:30 am–5:00 pm, Sun 11:00 am–5:00 pm

This building began as a church and residence in 1857 and was also used as a shoemaker's shop. (Note the sundial on the south exterior wall; it is one of only three sundials in the Colonies.) Today, Olde World Lace Shoppe occupies half of the building. It features curtains, tablecloths, place mats, runners, doilies, handkerchiefs, Victorian dolls, teddy bears, and gifts. Christmas table lace and linens are available, as are Austrian crystal, Belgian lace, and various craft products.

■ Oma's Haus [28]

Telephone: 319-622-3274
Hours: daily 10:00 am–5:00 pm

Oma's (grandmother's) Haus offers handmade gifts by area craftspeople. Angels and angel pins, Christmas items, Santas, wreaths, and unique gifts depicting animals, such as rabbit-shaped eggs, are available. This building was a woodshed and washhouse for an old communal kitchen and residence built in 1861–1862. The brick addition was built in 1884.

■ Powder House [16]

Telephone: 319-622-3100
Hours: Mon–Sat 9:00 am–5:00 pm, Sun 12:00 pm–5:00 pm

The Powder House offers a range of handcrafted wood items and gifts made on site. Two very popular items are wooden rollers that come with a list of 101 uses, and "personal photo mounts," which are unique, custom-made walnut frames. Send or bring in a photograph, and the artists at the Powder House will transform it into a gift. Ideas include family, wedding, and children's photographs as well as photographs of pets, cars, landscapes, and sporting events.

The building was originally a grinding mill, with a windmill temporarily attached to it, built around 1870. By 1915 the building was being used for mixing a livestock feed additive called hog powder. In 1932 it was utilized for storage by the telephone company and a local winery. Finally, in 1990 the building was restored, with a windmill attached, and rented as a craft shop.

In 1988, R.C. Eichacker, the proprietor, a peace activist, sent a letter to Soviet President Mikhail Gorbachev. This letter resulted in a joint U.S.-Soviet peace effort in the fields at the 1988 World Agriculture Expo, held in Amana. Outside the Powder House is the Peace Park, developed by Eichacker; it includes a peace pole urging, "May Peace Prevail on Earth" in four languages: English, Russian, Chinese, and German.

■ Red Fox Paper Den [55]

Telephone: 319-622-3212
Hours: Sun–Thu 9:00 am–5:00 pm, Fri–Sat 9:00 am–5:30 pm

The Paper Den is full of greeting cards, stationery, wrapping paper, invitations, napkins, rubber stamps, and accessories. Also available are English and German books and cards, cookbooks, stuffed animals, and toys. The shop is located next door to Maddie's/Der Laden Apparel and Gifts and across the parking lot from the Brick Haus Restaurant.

■ The Red Geranium [40]

Telephone: 319-622-3623
Hours: Mon–Thu 9:00 am–5:30 pm, Fri–Sat 9:00 am–6:00 pm, Sun 10:00 am–5:00 pm

This gift store offers a large selection of Yankee candles, floral arrangements, Lang and Mainstreet Press greeting cards, and gourmet coffees. The building is part of Noé House Inn, built as a communal residence in 1856 with additions in 1900 and 1904. It is believed to be the first gift shop in Amana and was formerly known as the Cellar Door.

■ Renate's Antique Gallery [13]

Telephone: 319-622-3859
Hours: Mon–Sat 10:00 am–5:00 pm, Sun 12:00 pm–5:00 pm

This 1870 communal home connects with Erenberger Antiques. Renate's features eight rooms of furniture, pottery, baskets, fabrics, and rugs on two levels. Look for the horseshoe on the sidewalk on your way into the store. "H.S." stands for Harold Shoemaker, the local blacksmith who built the railing in front.

■ Roger's Anvil/Industrial Machine Shop Museum [65]

Telephone: 319-622-3482
Hours: daily 9:00 am–5:00 pm

Roger and Delta Quaintance operate the Anvil, where Roger creates ironwork from a forge. He will make items to order, or shoppers can choose from any number of items on display including weathervanes, buckles, wall and ceiling hooks, fireplace tools, wall brackets, knives, dinner bells, boot scrapers, flowerpot rings, yard stands, curtain tiebacks, basket hangers, and more. This craftsman's work can be viewed in progress on many mornings.

■ Sandstone Winery [26]

Telephone: 319-622-3081/319-622-3709
Hours: daily 9:00 am–5:00 pm

This winery was established in 1960. The entire wine-making process is conducted on site. The tasting room is small but packs in many smooth fruit wines. Austrian lead crystal, German smokers, and nutcrackers are also available. The tasting room is located to the side and rear of this 1857 communal kitchen and residence that was once believed to be occupied by *Werkzeug* Christian Metz. For some time, Metz lived in the basement of the home, not wanting to occupy a house until all other villagers had secured homes.

■ Santa's Sleigh [24]

Telephone: 319-622-7663
Hours: Mon–Sat 8:30 am–6:00 pm, Sun 11:00 am–5:00 pm

Santa's Sleigh is the Amana General Store's Christmas shop. It is believed to have been built in 1860 as a watch house and basket shop. The sign out front states it was also an umbrella shop, chicken shed, holding shed, and warehouse. The building was a post office from 1942 to 1954. Now it delivers Christmas items and is loaded with Crinkle Claus figures, Possible Dreams, Villages by Lefton, Steinbach wooden ornaments, Old World Christmas glass ornaments, olive-wood ornaments from Bethlehem, and various collectibles and decorations.

■ Schnitzelbank [57]

Telephone: 319-622-3359
Hours: Mon–Sat 9:00 am–6:00 pm, Sun 11:00 am–5:00 pm

Schnitzelbank means "toys and gifts," and that's just what shoppers will find in this business connected to the Kitchen Sink. Toys, puzzles, board games, stuffed animals, Snowbabies, miniature figures, rubber stamps, collectibles, and personalized tapes are available. The building was a communal kitchen and residence and was built in 1872.

■ Smokehouse Square Antiques [9]

Telephone: 319-622-3539
Hours: Mon–Sat 9:30 am–5:30 pm, Sun 11:00 am–5:00 pm

Smokehouse Square offers wares from 30 different antique dealers on two spacious levels. The building was constructed in 1943 as a clubhouse for the Amana Welfare Association. It was designed to accommodate dances, movies, wedding receptions, card parties, picnics, and seasonal gatherings. Today the store offers stoneware, pottery, glassware, folk art, primitives, books, tools, furniture, quilts, and old advertising signs.

■ Tick Tock Antiques [38]

Telephone: 319-622-3730
Hours: Daily 10:00 am–4:00 pm

At Tick Tock, located across a driveway from the Ox Yoke Inn, visitors will find collectible plates, clocks, books, primitives, dishes, glass art, linens, needlework, tools, and select furniture. The shop is packed with many other antique and gift items as well. The Tick Tock building is believed to be a former garage for the adjacent Noé House, which is now an inn with three gift shops.

■ Tiny Tim's Colony Christmas [47]

Telephone: 319-622-6362
Hours: Mon–Fri 10:00 am–8:00 pm, Sat 9:00 am–8:00 pm,
   Sun 11:00 am–5:00 pm

One of Amana's many popular Christmas stores is Tiny Tim's, located in a former communal kitchen and residence built in 1856. It has a wide selection of trees, plates, statues, ornaments, angels, buttons, pins, reindeer, Frostys, sleighs, stuffed animals, handcarved Santas, personalized ornaments, Porter music boxes, CDs and cassettes, the Polanaise collection, Fontanini heirloom nativities, and nativities from around the world. Tiny Tim's proprietors also operate the Colony Gardens.

■ Village Leather Haus [20]

Telephone: 319-622-6088
Hours: Mon–Sat 10:00 am–5:00 pm, Sun 11:00 am–4:00 pm

Located across the street from the Ronneburg Restaurant, this 1857 communal kitchen and residence received a brick addition in 1900. It now houses the Village Leather Haus, featuring Southwest and Western ware, handmade belts, hats, purses, billfolds, moccasins, and wicker items such as baskets and brooms.

■ The Village Mall [19]

Telephone: 319-622-3742
Hours: Mon–Sat 10:00 am–5:00 pm, Sun 11:00 am–4:00 pm

The Village Mall offers ice cream, a variety of homemade fudges, and a number of gift items. The mall has a wide selection of lace goods including tablecloths, place mats, runners, and doilies. A back section houses dolls and doll houses, greeting cards, and some souvenir items. No date of origin is available for what appears to have been a communal residence.

■ Village Pastry Shop [14]

Telephone: 319-622-6498
Hours: Sun–Fri 7:30 am–5:00 pm, Sat 7:30 am–6:00 pm

The Village Pastry Shop offers baked goods, food and drink items, and gifts. Pastries, pies, homemade fudge, candy, breads, gourmet foods, coffee, and various Amana food products are available. Baked items include cinnamon rolls, pecan stickies, frosted donuts, muffins, iced sweet buns, strudel, turnovers, cookies, cheesecake, Snickers clusters, carrot cake, and black forest cake. Fudge flavors include, among others, rocky road and vanilla praline. Amana food products include local Millstream root beer, Millstream beer, and various Amana breads, jams, jellies, and sauerkraut. The shop also has a number of tables and chairs where visitors can sit to eat.

This building was constructed in 1867 and housed the pharmacy and doctor's office. In 1932, the doctor moved his office to the home across the street. That home is now the Museum of Amana History.

■ Village Tours and Guide Service

Telephone: 319-622-3269
Hours: vary, contact by phone

Village Tours provides guided tour services for all seven villages, with narrations covering local history, religion, and life in communal times. Tour duration is four hours plus an arranged meal at one of the local restaurants. Stops include the Amana Woolen Mill, a furniture factory, meat market, bakery, winery, and more. Tourists use their own vehicles and travel in a caravan.

■ Village Winery and Gift Gallery   [62]

Telephone: 319-622-3448/800-731-7142
Hours: Summer, Mon–Sat 9:00 am-5:30 pm, Sun 11:00 am–5:00 pm; otherwise daily 10:00 am-4:00 pm

This winery and gift gallery could be two separate stores. The winery offers tasting of 15 wines and also sells wine, beer, cheese, steins, and mugs. The gift shop offers a very large selection of collectibles including Hummels, Snowbabies, Snowbunnies, Jan Hagara, Anri woodcarvings, Cherished Teddies, Memories of Yesterday, David Winter cottages, Walt Disney classics, Lowell Davis farm club, Fenton art glass, Victoria Ashlea originals, dolls, stained glass villages, and a Christmas room with Belsuickle Santas, Enesco collectibles, and collectible ornaments.

East Amana

There are no commercial establishments in East Amana, but for the tourist or other visitor, it is a wonderful village through which to drive, bike, or walk. In East Amana, one can get a better feel for what the villages may have been like in earlier times. The breeze hugs the hillside and blows across the uncluttered streets. The pace seems slow and relaxing, with simplicity everywhere. Nearly all the homes are original to the village and have well-tended gardens and yards. Farm buildings line the roadway, just two miles from Amana.

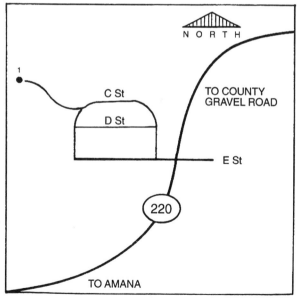

East Amana
1. Cemetery

Knitting School (Strickschule), *circa 1905. Boys also learned to knit, and children made their own winter stockings. (Photo courtesy Amana Heritage Society.)*

In the spring of 1860, East Amana became the sixth village settled. The primary reason for establishing East Amana was to accommodate sheep herds. Large herds were needed to supply wool for the nearby woolen mill in Amana. The area around East Amana was ideal due to its proximity to the woolen mill and to its rolling hills and available pastureland. The sheep herds were so large that a kitchen house was kept just for the sheep herders.

East Amana was laid out and operated like the other villages, with farm buildings at one end and shops at the other. The church, five communal kitchen houses, and communal residences were in the center of the settlement.

The village had a number of shops and buildings including a bakery, blacksmith, broom and basket shop, buggy shop, butcher, cabinet shop, carpenter, cooper or tinsmith, engine house, ice house, machine shed, molasses and sorghum factory, tailor, sawmill, school, watch house, and wagon shop.

Agricultural buildings in the village included a corncrib, a granary, and barns for colts, dairy cattle, hogs, horses, oxen, and sheep. The village also had a cherry orchard, bee houses for honey production, and a willow patch for basket-making.

The East Amana General Store occupied an old church building from 1932 to 1975. The church had been built in 1871. In 1940, East Amana was the first village to have all the homes wired for electricity. In 1943, the school closed and the children traveled to Amana for lessons.

A special place in East Amana is the village cemetery, located in the rear of the village, opposite the highway. A long lane, lined with pine trees, brings visitors to the hillside plots, which are guarded by towering pines on all sides. Rows of headstones, each stone much like the next, bespeak the simple way of life and death in the Colonies. Everyone was equal in the Community of True Inspiration, and in no place is that more clear than in the Amana cemeteries. In East Amana, the wind actually whistles

The peaceful hillside cemetery in East Amana. In death, as in life, all village members were considered equal. (Photo by author.)

through the trees and provides a reverent, serene environment in which to pay your respects and gather a sense of purpose.

Amana cemeteries are all similar. Located near the edge of the original village and lined with pine trees, the plots are laid out according to time of death. When a member dies, he or she is buried next to the last member who passed away, not with his or her family, as is the custom in many American communities. The headstones face east toward the sunrise, and are all the same: sandstone slabs rounded at the top, each displaying the name, date of death, and the person's age at death by year, month, and day. A wooden stake in the ground marks the site for the next burial. In the winter months during earlier times straw was placed on the ground in a few spots to make digging easier in the event of a death. Christian Metz, the Community's most influential *Werkzeug*, or inspired leader, is buried at the cemetery in the village of Amana.

High Amana

High Amana has an operating general store and the Amana Arts Guild Center. It provides visitors an opportunity to drive or walk through a quiet village and imagine what it was like 100 years ago.

As construction began in the spring of 1857, High Amana became the fourth village settled in the Colonies. Locating a sawmill between the villages of Amana and West Amana was the primary reason for developing High Amana. Rather than continuing to haul lumber from Amana to West Amana for building construction, a sawmill was created. The village grew around the sawmill operation.

Like the other villages, High Amana had farm buildings at one end of the settlement and shops at the other. A church, five communal kitchen houses, and communal residences were in the center of the village.

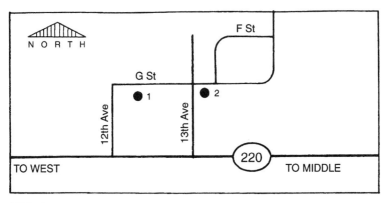

High Amana
1. Amana Arts Guild Center
2. Old Fashioned High Amana General Store

Henry and Louise Miller in the Amana Tannewald. *The Colonists planted pine groves, which were a favorite retreat. The federal government requested the groves be cut for wood during World War II. (Photo courtesy Amana Heritage Society.)*

Shops and buildings in High Amana included a blacksmith, broom shop, buggy and wagon shop, butcher, carpenter, drying house, general store, harness shop, ice house, pump house, sawmill, school, shoe shop, tailor, tannery, wagon shop, and an underground wine and beer cellar.

Agricultural buildings included an apiary, calf barn, colt barn, corncrib, cow barn, granary and tile works, hog house, and oxen barn. The village also had a fruit orchard and a willow patch for basket-making.

Shops and Tourist Attractions

■ Amana Arts Guild Center [1]

Telephone: 319-622-3678
Hours: May-Sept, Wed-Sun 10:30 am–4:00 pm (also open Mon-Tues 12:00 pm-4:00 pm early July-mid Aug); Oct, Sat-Sun 10:30 am-4:00 pm

The Amana Arts Guild Center preserves the arts and crafts of communal days by offering exhibits, displays, and craft demonstrations. Many items for sale are created by local artists, who have honed their skills in apprenticeships, as their ancestors did. Beautiful and superbly produced quilts, baskets, rugs, and other items are available in the gift shop. Amana- and Iowa-made dolls, prints, wood items, and unique collections, such as a number of ark reproductions made of gourds, are also available.

At the Arts Guild, visitors have the opportunity to watch

The Amana Arts Guild, home to creative arts demonstrations and exhibits. The building had been the village church and school and has a sundial on the exterior wall. (Photo by author.)

artists at work. Basket makers, using locally grown, peeled willows, create their beautiful products before your very eyes, as do quilters, lithographers, and tinsmiths. Check with the Arts Guild for the times of these demonstrations.

The building was originally a church built in 1858. The frame portion was the earliest school for High Amana. A sundial, one of only three in the Colonies, is located on the south exterior wall.

■ Old Fashioned High Amana General Store [2]

Telephone: 319-622-3797
Hours: Sun–Fri 10:00 am–5:00 pm, Sat 10:00 am–5:30 pm

This old-fashioned store has long aisles and exposed beams, and is in the same condition as it was in the early days. It retains original fixtures, counters, and a pressed-metal ceiling. A watchtower, since removed, was located on the top and west of the building. The store was built around 1858 to provide some supplies to the communal kitchens and various staples to village residents. You can still shop here for many food items as well as candy, kitchen items, crafts, prints, quilts, pottery, books, games, and gifts.

Homestead

Homestead has a very long street on which the restaurants, lodging facilities, and various shops are located. Former New York Yankee pitcher Bill Zuber's Dugout Restaurant provides family-style dining, and the Homestead Kitchen offers a homey diner environment popular with local residents. Die Heimat Country Inn offers 19 rooms for overnight visitors, and Rawson's Bed and Breakfast displays a wide assortment of antiques. Homestead

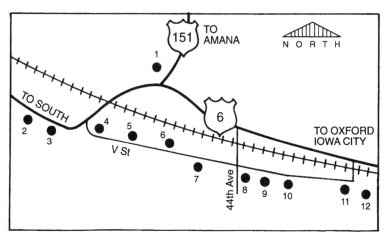

Homestead
1. Amana Colonies Nature Trail
2. Colony Country Store
3. Homestead Kitchen
4. Ehrle Brothers Winery
5. Alma's Washhouse
6. Amana Meat Shop and Smokehouse
7. Amana Community Church Museum
8. Bill Zuber's Dugout Restaurant
9. The Pepper Mill
10. Rawson's Bed and Breakfast
11. Die Heimat Country Inn
12. Homestead Cider Mill

Map numbers also appear beside the description of each establishment.

also has an operating meat shop and smokehouse, a well-preserved church museum, several shops, a winery, and a nature trail just outside of town which affords brisk (or leisurely) hikes in a beautiful environment.

Homestead began as a campsite in 1841 and developed into a stagecoach stop prior to the arrival of the Colonists from Ebenezer, New York. When the villagers realized a railroad would be placed through Homestead, they purchased the area in 1860 to develop a depot from which to ship their saleable products. Homestead was the fifth Amana village developed.

The newest Amana village was transformed into the style of the other villages, as buildings were either moved or constructed to provide for the needs of the community. Farm buildings were on one end of the village, and shops were at the other end. A church, nine communal kitchen houses, and communal residences were in the center of the village. A bridge was built across the Iowa river to connect Homestead with Amana.

Buildings and shops in Homestead included an ash house, bakery, basket shop, blacksmith, boiler house, brickyard, broom shop, butcher, community washhouse, cooper or tinsmith, carpenter, carpet weaver, depot, drying house, firehouse, general store, harness shop, hobo hotel, hotel, ice house, knitting-school house, locksmith, lumber shed, machine shop, press house, pump house, sawmill, school, shoe shop, wagon shop, watch house, and wood-chopping house. A doctor and pharmacy were also located in Homestead.

Agricultural buildings included a calf barn, a colt barn, a corncrib, a cow barn, a feed mill, a granary, a heifer barn, a hog barn, a grain elevator, an implement building, a milk station, and a steer barn. A willow patch and orchards were present, and the villagers constructed a pond for ice harvesting.

RESTAURANTS

■ Homestead Kitchen [3]*

■ QUICK FACTS
Telephone: 319-622-3203
Hours: Sun–Thu 7:30 am–8:00 pm, Fri–Sat 7:30–9:00 pm
Capacity: about 100 in two rooms
Groups: yes
Parking: plenty of parking in adjacent lot
Handicap accessible: yes
Smoking: in designated areas only
Price range: breakfast $2.50–$4.95, lunch $2.95–$5.50, dinner $7.25–$8.50
Payment methods: cash, check
Family-style dining: no
Children's menu: yes, items are listed in main menu

Bricks from the dismantled calico mill tower were used to build the Homestead Kitchen, a popular diner for local residents. (Photo by author.)

---
* The number refers to location on the village map.

Customer favorites: breakfast items, breaded pork tenderloin
Building: constructed 1934 as a sandwich shop
Restaurant opened: 1934
Host: Terry Davis

Originally built in 1934 as the Homestead Sandwich Shop, the Homestead Kitchen has the feel of a small-town diner. Prior to 1932, villagers ate in communal kitchen houses. When the Great Change of 1932 occurred, the communal kitchen houses closed, and villagers had to cook for themselves. Because the colonists had to build kitchens into their homes, many enjoyed the convenience of the Sandwich Shop. Carrying on this early post–Great Change function, the Homestead Kitchen is a favorite of both visitors and local residents. Many local residents still refer to the Kitchen as the Sandwich Shop or the Old Homestead Inn, both earlier names for the restaurant.

Many of the bricks used in the construction of the building came from the Amana Furniture Shop in Amana. The Furniture Shop was originally a calico mill which produced colored and patterned fabric. When the mill's tower was removed in 1934, the colonists, who weren't accustomed to wasting a resource, hauled the bricks to Homestead for the new sandwich shop.

Inside, the Homestead Kitchen has two carpeted dining rooms. The front dining room also has counter seating with rotating stools. Mugs and glasses line the wall behind the counter, and there are country themes and old-fashioned signs and prints on the walls. The rear dining room also has booths, tables, and prints which were purchased from the Amana Furniture Shop.

Sandwiches, platters, homemade soups, salads, and daily specials are popular. There are light meals available, and a children's menu is listed in the main menu. The restaurant serves about 100 homemade pies a week.

Customers fill the diner for breakfast, lunch, and dinner. A lunch and dinner favorite is the hand-breaded pork tenderloin, which is twice the size of its bun. Another favorite is the hot roast beef, which is served on fresh bread with mashed potatoes, brown gravy, and a side of cole slaw.

A small gift area offers mugs, books, postcards, and food items such as jams, jellies, mustard, sauerkraut, and candy. Carry-out soft drinks and beer are available.

■ MENU SAMPLE

Breakfast: blueberry pancakes; biscuits and gravy; French toast; omelets; rolls; muffins; and kitchen platters, which include eggs, grilled smoked pork chops with eggs, Amana ham and eggs, and steak and eggs and are served with hash browns and toast.

Appetizers: breaded corn nuggets, chicken livers, chicken strips, and spinach and cheese dynabites.

Lunch platters: include *Wiener Schnitzel* (breaded veal cutlet), grilled Amana ham steak, bratwurst, knockwurst, and smoked pork chops; served with potato, vegetable, cole slaw or gelatin, and bread and butter.

Lunch sandwich platters: include the Cyclone burger topped with grilled Amana ham and melted cheese and the Hawkeye Reuben with Amana ham, Swiss cheese, sauerkraut, and a special dressing; served with French fries and cole slaw.

Lunch baskets: include chicken strips, battered fish, shrimp, chicken, and fried chicken liver; served with French fries, cole slaw, and bread and butter.

Dinner items: *Wiener Schnitzel* (breaded veal cutlet), top sirloin, fried chicken, cod fillets, smoked pork chop, jumbo shrimp, steak and shrimp, and Amana ham; served with soup or salad, potato, vegetables, and bread and butter.

Children's menu: hamburger, cheeseburger, grilled cheese, fried fish, and chicken strips; served with French fries, gelatin, and drink.

Desserts: homemade pies such as apple, cherry, blueberry, and chocolate or coconut cream; strawberry, chocolate, or butterscotch ice cream sundaes; hand-dipped ice cream and sherbet; cheesecake; and chocolate pudding cake.

Beverages: soft drinks with free refills, coffee, tea, milk, hot chocolate, and lemonade.

Alcoholic beverages: local and other domestic wines, wine coolers, Millstream and other domestic beers, nonalcoholic beer, and Heineken.

■ Bill Zuber's Dugout Restaurant [8]

■ QUICK FACTS
Telephone: 319-622-3911/800-316-8353
Hours: Mon–Sat lunch 11:00 am–2:00 pm, dinner 4:30 pm–8:00 pm; Sun 11:00 am–7:30 pm
Capacity: 210
Groups: yes
Parking: in lot and on side street
Handicap accessible: yes
Smoking: no
Price range: lunch $2.50–$5.75, dinner $8.50–$14.00
Payment methods: cash, check, American Express, Discover, MasterCard, Visa
Family-style dining: yes
Children's menu: regular menu at reduced price
Customer favorites: oven-baked steak and country-fried chicken
Building: constructed circa 1862 as a hotel
Restaurant opened: 1949
Host: Terry Davis

Bill Zuber pitched for the World Champion New York Yankees before returning to the Colonies to open his restaurant. (Photo by author.)

Bill Zuber's Dugout Restaurant is named for the New York Yankee pitcher who opened the restaurant with his wife Connie in 1949 after Bill ended his major league career. After Bill's death in 1982, Connie continued to run the restaurant until her retirement in 1995.

It would seem extraordinary that a young man growing up in the Amana Colonies, where playing baseball was at first forbidden and later frowned upon, would emerge as a major league baseball pitcher. But then, Bill Zuber was not an ordinary person. Even though he didn't see a baseball game until he was 14 years old, he was discovered three years later by a major league scout and was on his way to an exciting career in the American League.

Born in 1913, Bill was a Middle Amana native. As the legend goes, he was recruited by a scout for the Cleveland Indians who had heard of his strong arm. When the scout came to see Zuber, there was no baseball. The scout picked up an onion and asked if Zuber could hit the nearby barn. Zuber took the onion and, instead of hitting the barn, threw it over the barn.

Zuber pitched for the 1943 World Champion New York Yankees, the 1946 American League Champion Boston Red Sox, the Cleveland Indians, and the Washington Senators. As a Senator in 1941, he pitched a 1–0 shutout of his future Yankee team, which included a line-up featuring DiMaggio, Selkirk, Dickey, Grodon, Henrich, Rizzuto, and Keller. Zuber compiled a record of 45–42 with 65 saves before returning home to enter the restaurant business.

The shape of the menu at Zuber's resembles a baseball and offers a number of items. Two popular meals are the oven-baked steak, nontenderized beef fillets slowly baked in gravy until fork tender; and the country-fried chicken, deep-fried and then baked for one and one-half hours, allowing the meat to fall off the bone. All of the meat is purchased from the Amana Meat Shop and Smokehouse in Homestead and Amana.

The main dining room is lined with photographs of the Amana Colonies and various sports figures. The Indian Dam dining room features various wildlife photographs and a large painting of the nearby Indian Dam in a more formal setting. The Wagon Wheel room is a rustic room of brick walls and a brick tile floor with wagon wheels hanging from the ceiling. Near the restroom is a colorful tile replica of a baseball diamond. The east dining room is decorated with antiques and is a favorite at Christmas time, when it beams with white tablecloths, candles, and holiday decorations.

The gift area includes baseball items such as small bats, mugs, magnets, and hats; candles; dolls; cards; and food items from the Colonies, including sauerkraut, breads, and beer.

Zuber's is filled with photographs and memorabilia of sports and entertainment celebrities including signed photographs of Bob Hope, Jayne Mansfield, Rocky Marciano, Jack Dempsey, Stan Musial, Yogi Berra, Joe DiMaggio, and Babe Ruth.

The Restaurant is believed to have been built in 1862 as a hotel and kitchen for travelers using the railroad at Homestead.

■ **MENU SAMPLE**

Appetizers: homemade soup and pickled ham.

Family-style dining: all dinners are served with refillable bowls of potato, vegetable, salad, cottage cheese, sauerkraut, bread and butter; and coffee, tea, or milk.

Dinner items: *Ofengebackenes Steak* (oven-baked steak), country-fried chicken, Amana *Wurst von Schweinefleish* (Amana seasoned pork sausage or bratwurst), *Wiener Schnitzel* (breaded veal cutlet), *Kassler Rippchen* (smoked pork chops), Amana ham, top sirloin, T-bone steak, porterhouse steak, jumbo breaded shrimp, and Friday night all-you-can-eat whole catfish.

Lunch plates: country-style chicken; Amana bratwurst; Amana ham; and sandwiches including beefburgers, cheese, grilled cheese, grilled chicken, Amana ham, Amana bratwurst, chicken, *Wiener Schnitzel*, and fish.

Desserts: homemade pies such as apple, rhubarb, chocolate or coconut cream, peach, and lemon meringue; ice cream, sherbet; chocolate sundae; and a special wine-sauce sundae.

Beverages: coffee, tea, milk, and soft drinks.
Alcoholic beverages: cocktails, local beer and wine, house and bottled wines, and domestic and imported beer including the German beers Dortmunder Actien, Beck's, and Hofbrau.

LODGING FACILITIES

■ Die Heimat Country Inn   [11]

■ QUICK FACTS
Telephone: 319-622-3937
Number of rooms: 19
Rate range: $45–$70
Payment methods: cash, check, MasterCard, Visa
Reservations: recommended, cancellations required by 9:00 am previous day
Check-in: flexible
Check-out: flexible
Private baths: yes
Amenities: air-conditioning, television (no cable), handpieced quilts
Breakfast: full breakfast
Parking: large lot in rear of building
Handicap accessible: lower level rooms available, short stairs to enter building
Smoking: no
Children: yes
Pets: three rooms accommodate pets
Building: constructed circa 1858 as a roadside inn
Inn opened: 1962
Hosts: Jacki and Warren Lock

With 19 rooms, Die Heimat Country Inn is the largest inn available in the seven villages and is a popular choice for those traveling in large numbers. Die Heimat is believed to have been built around 1858 as a roadside inn on the stagecoach line. In 1862, the Colonies purchased the existing village of Homestead to obtain access to the new railroad. From 1906 to 1932, the building was used as a communal kitchen house. From 1932 to 1962, it was a private residence. In 1962, an inn was opened.

Since its opening in 1962, the Inn has changed hands a few times. In 1993, Warren and Jacki Locke purchased the Inn. Jacki is from the Midwest, and Warren is a former tennis pro from Australia. Jacki says that she and Warren love to meet and talk with people, and their mixture of Aussie personality and Midwestern friendliness is a perfect fit for this people-oriented business.

The rooms at Die Heimat (the home place) have Amana walnut and cherry furniture and various heirlooms. Handpieced quilts cover most of the beds, and original oil lamp fixtures are on the walls. Amana carpets cover the wide plank floors. The 19 rooms offer a variety of accommodations, with queen-, double-, and two-double-bed arrangements. Jacki encourages guests to call and tell her their needs, and she will fit them into the right room. Ten rooms are on the ground level and nine are on the second level. On the ground level are three rooms which can all adjoin and which work well for families. Each of the three rooms has two double beds, a full bath, table and chairs, small refrigerator, and comforters rather than quilts. Cribs for infants are available.

Five of the Inn's rooms have canopy beds made in the Amana Furniture Shop. Guests can choose beds with either a flat or a curved canopy. These beds are available in either queen or double size. These rooms also have Amana grandfather or grandmother rockers.

All rooms have hand-pierced lamp shades, which Jacki also sells. The color Amana blue, which is common in the villages, is seen throughout the Inn. Early Amana Colony photographs decorate the maze of walls throughout the Inn.

The Inn has a large backyard for lawn croquet and an Amana lawn swing and is only a few hundred yards from the Amana Colonies nature trail. The trail offers brisk walks and an overlook of an early-period Native American fishing dam (known locally as the Indian Dam) on the Iowa River.

The Inn can accommodate 40 people and is popular as a mini-

This curved canopy bed at Die Heimat Country Inn was made at the Amana Furniture Shop. (Photo by author.)

retreat for family reunions, off-site business meetings, and church or education groups. Die Heimat offers getaway packages which include meals at the Colony Inn Restaurant in Amana. It also conducts murder mystery weekends during the winter months.

A full, hot breakfast is served in the parlor/lobby area from 7:45 am to 9:30 am. A typical breakfast includes scrambled eggs, French toast sticks, breakfast pizza, fruit, orange and tomato juice, and coffee.

The lobby offers a large area for eating and lounging. The room has an Amana grandfather clock, three Amana-style couches, two coffee tables, two tables and chairs, and a buffet. Guests can select a board game or reading material, and card playing is a favorite pastime of many guests.

■ Rawson's Bed and Breakfast [10]

■ QUICK FACTS
Telephone: 319-622-6035/800-637-6035
Number of rooms: five
Rate range: $45–$75
Payment methods: cash, check, MasterCard, Visa
Reservations: recommended
Check-in: after 2:00 pm
Check-out: 11:00 am
Private baths: in four of five rooms
Amenities: air-conditioning, remote control television, antique furnishings
Breakfast: continental breakfast
Parking: in front
Handicap accessible: no, all rooms on upper level
Smoking: no
Pets: no
Building: constructed 1858 as a communal kitchen
Inn opened: 1989
Hosts: Janice and Rick Rawson

Rawson's Bed and Breakfast, an 1858 communal kitchen house, is now furnished with eclectic pieces. (Photo by author.)

Rawson's Bed and Breakfast offers five distinct bedrooms for guests, and the home is filled with unique and entertaining antique pieces. Janice Rawson, a former special education teacher, and her husband, Rick, have worked hard to prepare the Inn for guests. They gutted and restored nearly 5,000 square feet of living space and filled it with their antique finds.

The five rooms include a whirlpool suite with a double bed, a three-room suite with a queen bed and daybed, two rooms with a double bed and a twin bed, and an overflow room with a double bed. A rollaway is available upon request.

The ground floor consists of two dining rooms and a guest parlor. The comfortable, dark parlor is decorated with an imported English floral wallpaper, an Amana couch, a piano, two slipper chairs surrounding an ornate table, a curio cabinet from Egypt, and an Amana hidden desk which is one of only seven such pieces made. Janice says, "I like different, unusual, one-of-a-kind pieces. I like to create interest areas for guests, to visually entertain them."

The popular whirlpool suite, features a 120-gallon whirlpool. The room has white walls with a dark floral border that matches the window treatments, bedspread, and even the decorative hat boxes found on the wardrobe. The double bed is on a lavish black and gold Victorian iron frame. The bathroom has a shower unit.

The three-room suite has a master bedroom with a queen bed. It features Amana pieces such as a trunk and a rocker, as well as European antiques such as the wardrobe. The blue carpet accents the red brick walls. The connecting room has a daybed. The full bath has a tub/shower.

Two other rooms in the inn are similar. They both have a double bed and a twin bed, which works well for families. They include a wardrobe, chairs, and light blue walls. One has a private bath, and the other has a bath across the hallway.

The overflow room is called Rose's Room and shares the bathroom across the hallway. Rose's Room is decorated with a dark green floral wallpaper against a ruby-colored carpet. It has a double bed, a wicker loveseat and table, and a small skylight. Janice's mother was born in the bed.

A light, sit-down breakfast varies but usually includes homemade blueberry streusel muffins or coffeecake, fruit platter, cereals, and juice, milk, coffee, or hot tea. The brick breakfast room has two dining tables in this old communal kitchen house.

Rawson's has won awards from several publications including a listing as one of *Newsweek* magazine's top bed and breakfast inns and the *Cedar Rapids Gazette*'s People's Choice Award as one of the top four inns in eastern Iowa. Janice says readers have responded to these articles. There was even a long-distance reservation from a couple in Scotland who had read about the Inn.

Janice's mother, Betty Peterson, operates Rose's Place Bed and Breakfast in Middle Amana. Rose was Janice's grandmother. In addition to running the Inn, Janice and Rick are busy with antique furniture collecting and craft shows, and they sell antique-reproduction doll furniture.

Shops and Tourist Attractions

■ Alma's Washhouse [5]

Telephone: 319-622-3606
Hours: Mon–Sat 9:00 am–5:00 pm, Sun 11:00 am–5:00 pm

This old communal washhouse offers factory-direct pottery, antiques, collectibles, and gifts. The pottery and stoneware is lead free, microwave safe, and made in the United States. Pieces include mugs, pitchers, pans, crocks, cereal bowls, soup bowls, pizza stones, and more. Antique dishes and spools are available.

In the old washhouses, items would be washed, hung in the attics of homes to dry, and then ironed. The iron was so heavy that, as one of Alma's clerk's says, "They thought they had arthritis, but it was really tendinitis." Soap for cleaning was produced in the ash house, using ashes from the kitchens and bakeries.

■ Amana Community Church Museum [7]

Telephone: 319-622-3567
Hours: open May–Oct, Mon–Sat 10:00 am–5:00 pm, Sun 12:00 pm–5:00 pm

The church was built in 1865 and acquired by the Amana Heritage Society in 1994 as a museum. Guides explain the religious traditions of the Community of True Inspiration, the architectural style of the church, and present-day practices. The Church is still active, and services are held each Sunday in the Middle Amana Church, with a German service at 8:30 am and an English service at 10:00 am. See the Middle Amana Church listing in the chapter on Middle Amana for more information on the church service. For additional information, see the section on religious beliefs under A History of the Amana Colonies in the first chapter.

■ Amana Colonies Nature Trail [1]

Telephone: none
Hours: open year-round for hiking

The nature trail offers plenty of hiking opportunities, a Native American dam and fish trap, and Native American burial grounds. The four interconnecting hiking trails through the outdoor scenery of the Iowa River valley offer hikes between one and three miles long. Bird-watchers will find a variety of winged wonders including bald eagles and wild turkey. Wildlife is abundant along the trail, and deer sightings are common. Numerous species of trees and wild flowers also await the hiker.

The dam is believed to have been constructed around 1200 A.D. by late woodland Sauk or Fox. The only fish trap of its kind in Iowa, the dam is included in the Iowa State Preserves System and is listed on the National Register of Historic Places. Boulders were utilized to build a barrier which guided the fish into a small pool where they were more easily caught. Since the construction of the Coralville reservoir near Iowa City, much of the dam is often under water.

Along the trail, a grouping of three Native American burial mounds can be found. These graves are believed to be 1,000 years old.

■ Amana Meat Shop and Smokehouse [6]

Telephone: 319-622-3931/800-373-6328
Fax: 800-373-3710
Hours: Mon–Sat 8:30 am–5:00 pm, all year; also open Sun 10:00 am–3:00 pm, May–Oct

The smell of hickory smoke fills the room as visitors enter the Amana Meat Shop and Smokehouse. For sale are Amana meat products including ham, sausage, bacon, pork chops, steaks, roasts, and bratwurst. Other items include cheese, breads, noodles, jellies, syrup, horseradish, and various gift items such as blankets, books, and coffee mugs.

The building was constructed around 1868 as a meat market and butcher shop, and meat products have always been produced in it, first for the communal kitchens and now for shoppers and local residents. The smoke tower was built in 1869. Adjacent is a small drying house which was used to dry fruits and vegetables for storage.

The smokehouse process involves starting a fire using green hickory wood cut from nearby forests. The meat is hung on hooks inside the three-story tower, and as the smoke rises to the cupola, the meat acquires its hickory-smoked flavor. The process takes three to seven days. Samples are available, and a catalog can be taken home to place orders. The only other remaining, operating meat shop in the Colonies is located in Amana.

■ Colony Country Store [2]

Telephone: 319-622-3197
Hours: Mon–Fri 9:00 am–5:00 pm, Sat–Sun 9:00 am–5:30 pm

Built as a gas station in 1932, the Colony Country Store now fills up travelers with a variety of food and drink items, clothing, books, kitchen items, and other gifts. Amana products such as meat, beer, and wine are available.

■ Ehrle Brothers Winery [4]

Telephone: 319-622-3241
Hours: Mon–Sat 9:00 am–5:00 pm, Sun 11:00 am–5:00 pm

The original and oldest winery in the Colonies is Ehrle Brothers, operated by Alma Ehrle, who once appeared on the television show "To Tell the Truth." She gave the audience quite a surprise when the host asked, "Will the real winemaker please stand up?"

The winery building was constructed around 1860 as a communal kitchen and residence and was purchased in 1932 by the Ehrle family. The winery was opened in 1934 by Alma's husband and his brother. The store offers gifts, cheese, sausage, other food items, and 12 varieties of wines including grape, rhubarb, cherry, apple, blueberry, raspberry, and dandelion. Erhle Brothers is also the home of the original "Lover's Wine," made from the Amana Church recipe.

Visitors to Ehrle Brothers can stroll through the wine cellar and note the distinctive aromas of aging fruit wine.

■ Homestead Cider Mill [12]

Telephone: 319-622-3694
Hours: open 24 hours with self-serve cooler

Fresh apple cider is available at the Homestead Cider Mill. Located in an old tinsmith shop, the Cider Mill presses the apples on site and offers samples or cider to go, from one glass to a gallon. Caramel apples are also often available as are seasonal Indian corn, pumpkins, squash, and fresh apples. There are also a few gift items and a line of Watkins products and Stanley Fuller brushes.

■ The Pepper Mill [9]

Telephone: 319-622-3897
Hours: Mon–Sat 9:00 am–6:00 pm, Sun 12:00 pm–4:00 pm, or knock at house

Built in 1864 as a communal kitchen and residence, the Mill operates from the old woodshed and washhouse. The Pepper Mill offers shoppers bulk herbs and spices, saltless seasonings, teas, dried vegetables and other edible products, essential oils, aroma therapy, and, of course, pepper mills.

Middle Amana

Middle Amana has two bed and breakfast choices; a family bakery; a pizza and burger restaurant; an 18-hole, professional golf course with a restaurant and condominium rentals; and a museum that features a well-preserved communal kitchen and cooper shop with informative tour guides.

Middle Amana was established in 1862 and was the last of the villages developed. Many of the Colonists who had remained the longest in the Community's former settlement at Ebenezer, New York, relocated to Middle Amana. The first structures were made of wood, but most of the later buildings were made of bricks produced from local clay. The last home was built in 1913.

The village was constructed with agricultural buildings at the east end and a shop street on the north. In the center of the village were a church, 10 communal kitchen houses, and communal residences.

The shops and buildings in the village included an ash house, bakery, basket shop, blacksmith, bookbindery, broom shop, butcher, cabinet shop, carpenter, carpet weaver, coal shed, cooper or tinsmith, cornstarch mill, fire station, garden house, harness shop, ice house, lumber shed, press house, print shop, sawmill, school, shoemaker, tailor, tank house, wagon shop, and watch house. A pharmacy, a doctor's office, and a general store were located along the southern border of the village.

A woolen mill and the machine shop were located near the millrace, which cut through the edge of town and provided a source of power for the mill. The Amana Refrigeration Company now occupies this location.

Agricultural buildings included a calf barn, cow barn, hog barn, horse barn, oxen barn, and steer barn. A sandstone quarry was nearby, and orchards and gardens were opposite the farming and shop sections of the village.

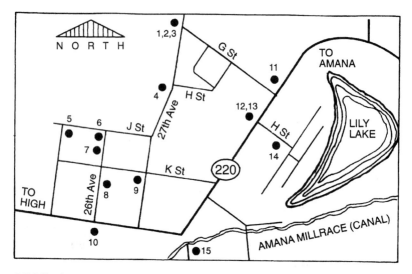

Middle Amana
1. Amana Colonies Golf Course
2. Player's Grill/Amana Colonies Golf Course
3. Amana Colonies Golf Course Condominiums
4. Amana Community Park
5. Hahn's Hearth Oven Bakery
6. Communal Kitchen and Coopershop Museum
7. Rose's Place Bed and Breakfast
8. Middle Amana Church
9. Dusk to Dawn Bed and Breakfast
10. Pizza Factory and Grill
11. Lakeview Village Retirement Community
12. Amana Community Library
13. Amana Community Pool
14. Colony Dolls
15. Amana Refrigeration

Map numbers also appear beside the description of each establishment.

Restaurants

■ Pizza Factory and Grill [10]

■ Quick Facts
Telephone: 319-622-3663
Hours: Sun 4:00 pm–8:00 pm, Mon–Thu 11:00 am–9:00 pm, Fri–Sat 11:00 am–9:30 pm
Capacity: 75
Groups: yes
Parking: in front of building
Handicap accessible: yes
Smoking: eating area is all smoking
Price range: appetizer $1–$3, entrees and pizza $3–$14
Payment methods: cash, check
Family-style dining: no
Children's menu: no
Customer favorites: all-you-can-eat pizza
Building: constructed 1870 as a general store
Restaurant opened: 1985
Host: Terry Davis

This 1870 village store is now the Pizza Factory and Grill. (Photo by author.)

The Pizza Factory and Grill is one of the few restaurants in Amana where visitors will find something other than German and family-style food. As the name implies, this is a pizza restaurant with a grill that sends out charbroiled burgers and sandwiches.

Built in 1870 as the Middle Amana General Store, the interior consists of a large, open room with a number of diner-style tables and chairs on linoleum flooring. From the menu on the wall, guests place orders at a counter. A condiment table and drink fountain are adjacent to the counter.

The Pizza Factory offers an all-you-can-eat buffet on Mondays from 5:00 pm to 8:00 pm and Fridays from 11:30 am to 1:00 pm. The Factory Special combo pizza is a popular item on the menu. Another choice, for adventurous patrons, is the German Favorite, which features Amana bratwurst smothered with sauerkraut and onions.

The building housed the general store from 1870 to 1985. It then became a pizza restaurant. The proprietor, Terry Davis, took over the restaurant in 1990. Davis also operates the Homestead Kitchen and Bill Zuber's Dugout Restaurant, both in Homestead. Terry says he gets quite a bit of local business, especially from workers at the nearby Amana Refrigeration plant.

■ MENU SAMPLE

Appetizers: chicken wings, mozzarella sticks, and broccoli cheese dynabites.

Pizza: thin or thick crust; taco, vegetable, bacon cheese, German Favorite (Amana bratwurst, sauerkraut, and onions), and Factory Special (combo).

Grill and sandwich items: charbroiled hamburgers, cheeseburgers, tenderloins, grilled chicken, and ham or turkey subs.

Beverages: soft drinks, coffee, tea, and lemonade.

Alcoholic beverages: domestic beer including local Millstream beer.

■ Player's Grill Restaurant / Amana Colonies [2]
Golf Course

■ QUICK FACTS
Telephone: 319-622-6224
Hours: Tue–Sat 11:00 am–8:00 pm, Sun–Mon 11:00 am–7:00 pm
Capacity: 150
Groups: yes, catering also available
Parking: adjacent lot
Handicap accessible: yes
Smoking: not permitted in restaurant
Price range: lunch and dinner $4.75–$6.95
Payment methods: cash, check, American Express, MasterCard, Visa
Concession counter: open during golf hours
Family-style dining: no
Children's menu: no
Building: constructed 1989, as a clubhouse for the golf course
Restaurant opened: 1989
Owner: private company

Player's Grill Restaurant is located in the clubhouse of the Amana Colonies Golf Course, an 18-hole, professional course with nearby condominium rentals. The restaurant is adjacent to the pro shop and offers grilled items, as well as soups and salads, for lunch and dinner.

Player's Grill has a modern interior, and guests can sit at tables or the bar, which offers a complete line of cocktails, domestic and imported beer, and wine. The Restaurant also has a lower level to accommodate groups, private meetings, or social gatherings. Dining and socializing is available indoors or on the deck which overlooks the golf course and the Middle Amana pond. The deck is spacious and wraps around two sides of the clubhouse.

A concession counter is also in the clubhouse and is open during course hours for beverages, snacks, sandwiches, and meals.

■ MENU SAMPLE
Appetizers: chicken quesadillas, chicken wings, nachos, mozzarella cheese bites, and jalapeño poppers.

Deli and sandwiches items: club, tuna or chicken salad, hamburger, patty melt, pork tenderloin, Philly steak, chicken melt, chicken fajita, and reuben sandwiches; soups; and salads.

Beverages: soft drinks, lemonade, iced tea, coffee, and hot chocolate.

Alcoholic beverages: full-service bar with canned and bottled domestic and imported beer, locally produced Millstream beer, local and other domestic wines, and mixed drinks.

Lodging Facilities

■ Amana Colonies Golf Course Condominiums [3]

■ **Quick Facts**
Telephone: 319-622-6222/800-383-3636
Number of rooms: nine
Rate range: $65–$135 for one bedroom, $110–$185 for two bedrooms, depending on length of stay and season
Payment methods: cash, check, American Express, MasterCard, Visa
Reservations: recommended
Check-in: 3:00 pm
Check-out: 11:00 am
Private baths: yes
Amenities: air-conditioning, cable television, and complete kitchen, fully furnished
Breakfast: no

Modern, fully-furnished condominiums offer all the amenities at the Amana Colonies Golf Course. (Photo by author.)

Handicap accessible: units are accessible, bedrooms and bathrooms are not
Smoking: in some units
Children: yes
Pets: no
Buildings: constructed 1990 as condominiums for golf course
Year opened: 1990
Owner: privately owned

The Amana Colonies Golf Course offers fully furnished condominiums on the edge of an 18-hole, professional golf course cut into a hardwood forest. Condominium rentals are available both to golfers using the course and to the general public. The condominiums offer screened-in porches with scenic views of the golf course and the heavily wooded area.

Four two-bedroom units and five single-bedroom units are available. The living room is carpeted and has couches and chairs, a coffee table, fireplace, cable television with remote control, a vaulted ceiling, and a ceiling fan. A small counter and bar-stool area connects to the kitchen, which contains a sink, dishwasher, stove and oven, microwave oven, full-size refrigerator, and coffeemaker. The fully stocked cabinets contain plates, glasses, and flatware.

The bedrooms are located in the lower level. A queen bed with dresser, nightstand with clock radio, full bath, and a washer and dryer unit are included. The bathroom is stocked with towels and the bedroom with extra sheets and blankets. There are windows in the bedroom and a walk-out, ground-level patio which leads to a walkway and the golf course. Both levels have closets and storage units, and a vacuum cleaner is included.

All guests need to bring is food and clothes. Golf clubs are available for rent at the course.

■ Dusk to Dawn Bed and Breakfast [9]

■ QUICK FACTS
Telephone: 319-622-3029/800-669-5773
Number of rooms: seven
Rate range: $50–$60
Payment methods: cash, check, American Express, Discover, MasterCard, Visa
Reservations: recommended, 48-hour notice required to cancel for full refund
Check in: 2:00 pm
Check out: 10:30 am
Private baths: yes
Amenities: air-conditioning, television, common deck area with outdoor Jacuzzi whirlpool, bicycles available for use
Breakfast: continental breakfast in two dining rooms
Parking: in front and at side
Handicap accessible: yes

At the Dusk to Dawn Bed and Breakfast, the outdoor Jacuzzi area connects the four-bedroom guest house with the three-bedroom main house. (Photo by author.)

Smoking: in patio area only
Children: yes
Pets: can make arrangements
Building: constructed 1862 as a communal residence
Inn opened: 1996 with current owners
Hosts: Jane and Gary Boesenberg

Dusk to Dawn has become a popular choice for families and guests traveling in groups. The inn offers seven rooms in two buildings which are connected by an exterior patio area featuring a Jacuzzi whirlpool.

The main house is a former communal residence built in 1862. From the patio area, guests can walk up the outside stairway to the bedrooms. At the top of the stairs is a small patio which is ideal for viewing stars and taking in the night air.

The upstairs area has three rooms with window air conditioners, ceiling fans, and color television with cable. Two of the rooms have full-size beds with antique headboards. A partitioned bathroom has a shower unit. The third room is a double room and has two full-size beds, a full bath, and a full-length, three-panel, department-store-style mirror with a wood frame. A kitchen and sitting area connects the three rooms and has a large, expandable dinner table for breakfast or games. The sitting area offers a rocker and an old-style Amana couch.

The guest house is on the ground level and has four rooms. Doors open to the street and the patio area. Jane says families and golfing guests especially enjoy the guest house accommodations, with their privacy, easy street access, and soothing Jacuzzi. The common kitchen area has a sink and a microwave and is furnished with a breakfast table and chairs, an Amana-style couch, and various antiques.

Bedrooms on the ground level consist of four rooms, two with full-size beds and full baths, and two with single beds and a shower unit. All four rooms are carpeted, and three have cable television The adjoining small sunroom has a table and chairs and a variety of games such as backgammon. An outdoor stereo system operates next to the Jacuzzi, which is available 24 hours.

A continental breakfast consists of baked goods such as coffee cake, rolls, or muffins and fresh fruit, juice, coffee, tea, and cocoa.

For the exercise enthusiast or those wanting a relaxing alternative to the automobile, bicycles are available. A new bike path from Middle Amana to Amana is scheduled to be constructed in 1998. Gift certificates are available from the inn.

■ Rose's Place Bed and Breakfast [7]

■ QUICK FACTS
Telephone: 319-622-6097
Number of rooms: three
Price range: $50
Payment methods: cash, check, MasterCard, Visa
Reservations: recommended, 24-hour cancellation policy
Check-in: after 2:00 pm
Check-out: by 11:00 am
Private baths: yes

The spacious red brick dining room at Rose's Place Bed and Breakfast. (Photo by author.)

Amenities: air-conditioning, color television, queen beds
Breakfast: full breakfast
Parking: in front
Handicap accessible: no, all bedrooms are upstairs
Smoking: outside only
Children: yes
Pets: no
Building: constructed 1884; believed to be a children's church and prayer meeting room which was later used as a Sunday school
Inn opened: 1993
Hosts: Betty and Jerry Peterson

Rose's Place Bed and Breakfast offers spacious guest rooms with queen-size beds, but the large dining and sitting room filled with antique furniture pieces is perhaps the most striking part of the home. An old wall was removed to create a grand room with an exquisite brick background. A large rug partially covers the original wood floor. Two breakfast tables with chairs are available in the dining room. The tables, a buffet, and two china cabinets are pieces from Betty's family. The sitting area has a wicker couch, chairs, a coffee table, and a piano. Crisp lace curtains hang on the brick-frame windows and accent the deep brick colors.

The three upstairs rooms are modern and spacious. All have queen beds, private baths with showers, color television, and air-conditioning. Chairs or rockers help fill the carpeted rooms, each of which is decorated in a different color scheme.

Betty named the inn after her mother and has placed many of her mother's and grandmother's furniture pieces throughout the house. Betty's daughter Janice operates Rawson's Bed and Breakfast in Homestead, and Janice calls one of her rooms Rose's Room.

Betty likes to visit with guests and enjoys cooking, often choosing the breakfast menu after she wakes up in the morning. For breakfast, guests are treated to baked goods from the family-operated Hahn's Hearth Oven Bakery, located nearby. These baked goods include cinnamon rolls, coffee cake, and kolaches. Betty also offers ham, French toast, seasonal fruits, cereals, coffee, hot tea, orange juice, and milk.

The inn building is believed to have been built as a children's church and prayer meeting room, and later used as a Sunday school. There are two items in the home that were used in the Sunday school: an 1890 piano, which guests are welcome to play, and a blackboard, which Betty uses at the entrance to mark guests' names and remind them of the time for breakfast.

If the weather is suitable, guests are welcome to relax and enjoy the outdoors in the backyard, where a table and chairs are available.

Rose's Place is adjacent to the Communal Kitchen and Coopershop Museum and is only one mile from the Amana Colonies Golf Course. Getaway packages in conjunction with the Colony Inn Restaurant are available. These include an overnight stay at Rose's and meals at the Colony Inn Restaurant in Amana.

Shops and Tourist Attractions

■ Amana Colonies Golf Course [1]

Telephone: 319-622-6222 or 319-622-6224/800-383-3636

The Amana Colonies Golf Course is an 18-hole, professional golf course with a clubhouse restaurant overlooking the course and nearby condominium rentals. The course is open mid-March through November, depending on the weather. Golfers can use the course from 6:30 am to 9:00 pm. The clubhouse has a full-service pro shop, club rentals, complete locker-room facilities, bag storage, and a driving range.

Over 30,000 rounds of golf are played on the course each year. The course is cut out of a hardwood forest on rolling hills and features watered, bent-grass fairways, five sets of tees, and a number of challenging water hazards and bunkers, including 64 sand traps. *Golf Magazine* tabbed the course as one of the "Top Ten Best New Public Courses in the Country" in 1990.

Playing the sprawling 300-acre course requires a golf cart, and the course has an 80-cart fleet. There are also four club pros to assist in improving the golfer's game. It is common for golfers to see some wildlife, such as deer and wild turkey, on the course.

A round of golf on this daily-fee course ranges from $28 to $55 depending on the number of holes played and on the day and time one plays. The fee includes tax and cart rental. Proper golf attire is required, shorts length is mid-thigh, shirts must have a collar, and tank tops are not allowed.

■ Amana Community Library [12]

Telephone: 319-622-3192
Hours: Mon 8:00 am–3:30 pm, Tue–Thu 8:00 am–7:00 pm, Fri 8:00 am–5:30 pm, Sat 9:00 am–12:00 pm

The lending libary is connected to the community school building and is open to the public.

■ Amana Community Park [4]

Telephone: none
Hours: accessible year-round

This spacious park has restrooms and offers camping without electrical hookup for $3 per night or with electrical hookup for $4 per night. A large soccer field can also be used for other sports.

The park is home to the annual bluegrass festival in July and the Amana Festival of the Arts in August. The covered Oktoberfest Pavilion provides shelter and picnic tables for gatherings. A second shelter and a service building are also available for use. The park was first utilized around 1921, and the restrooms and shelters were built in the 1960s.

■ Amana Community Pool [13]

Telephone: 319-622-3792
Hours: public swimming Sun 2:00 pm–4:00 pm, Wed and Fri 7:00 pm–9:00 pm; aerobics Tue and Thu 8:00 am–9:00 am; lap swim Mon–Fri 6:00 am–7:00 am

The pool is located in the community school building and features a diving board, showers, and lockers. Swim fee is $1.75 for adults, $1 for students, and 25 cents for preschool children.

■ Amana Refrigeration [15]

Telephone: 319-622-5511
Hours: not open to the public

Although this facility is not open to the public, travelers can't miss the factory as they round the bend in Middle Amana. Amana Refrigeration makes a full line of washers, dryers, refrigerators, air conditioners, and microwave ovens.

The company has its roots in Amana. In 1934, native son George Foerstner was asked to make a beverage cooler for a local businessman. This idea sprouted a line of freezers, and the company was off and running. The company set up shop in the former Middle Amana woolen mill complex, which was first developed in 1863, but abandoned as a mill operation shortly after the Great Change in 1932. The company merged with Raytheon in 1965, and this merger led to the production of the Amana microwave oven. In 1997, Raytheon planned to sell the company to Goodman Holding Company, of Houston, a manufacturer of heating and air-conditioning equipment. The 100-acre complex is a major employer in the region with over 2,800 employees. The plant's products are available at the Amana General Store in Amana.

■ Colony Dolls [14]

Telephone: 319-622-3020
Hours: Mon–Fri 9:00 am–5:00 pm, Sat 9:00 am–5:00 pm, Sun 12:00 pm–5:00 pm

A wide selection of porcelain dolls are hand painted, signed, and dated by local artists. Doll-making supplies and classes are also available. Colony Dolls is located in a modern-era garage.

■ Communal Kitchen and Coopershop Museum [6]

Telephone: 319-622-3567
Hours: open May–Oct, Mon–Sat 9:00 am–5:00 pm, Sun 12:00 pm–5:00 pm

Middle Amana

This original 1863 communal kitchen house is the only intact kitchen remaining in the villages. It is now a museum offering tours. (Photo by author.)

This museum features the only intact communal kitchen house remaining in the Colonies. Built in 1863, the museum appears as it did when the communal kitchens closed in 1932. From 1863 until 1932, village residents ate their meals together in these communal kitchens. Individual homes did not have kitchens.

The kitchen museum includes a brick hearth, dry sink, and various kitchen tools. The dining room is set with china and silver and looks as if a meal is ready to be served.

Each village had several kitchen houses, with a total of nearly 60 kitchen houses in all of the villages. Five meals a day were served to the 30–45 villagers assigned to each kitchen. A female kitchen boss directed the operation with help from at least three women who rotated the weekly duties of preparing vegetables, cooking, and washing dishes.

The village bakery would deliver breads and other baked goods, the meat shop would bring the available meats, and the dairy barn would deliver the milk and butter. Ice harvested during the winter and stored in insulated ice houses was also delivered.

Additional kitchen help tended the large vegetable gardens which provided the bulk of the food items. Canning and preserving was an enormous task necessary to provide food during the winter months.

During meals, men and women sat at separate tables, a prayer opened and closed the meal with little talking in between. Villagers were expected to finish their food and continue with the day's work.

The meals followed a weekly menu and varied slightly during different seasons to accommodate items that were available. Pages 22-23 in the first chapter shows a typical weekly menu. The villagers had plenty to eat, and despite the methodical schedule, there was a fair amount of variety.

Across the street from the kitchen house is the Coopershop Museum. The cooper shop was built around 1863 and provided metal items for the village including buckets, tubs, and barrels to hold food and water.

An admission fee of $1.50 for adults and 75 cents for children over eight is charged. A combination ticket for the four Amana Heritage Society Museums is available.

■ Hahn's Hearth Oven Bakery [5]

Telephone: 319-622-3439
Hours: from 7:30 am until baked goods are sold: Apr–Oct, Tue–Sat; Mar, Nov, and Dec, Wed and Sat only; Jan–Feb, Sat only

This original community bakery and residence was built in 1864. Jack and Doris Hahn carried on the tradition of the German hearth-oven bakery until Jack passed away in 1997.

Now, Doris bakes all the bread, coffee cake, and rolls sold here. Doris's sister, Pat Bahr, who also assists with the baking, will be happy to prepare a mouth-watering homemade pie per your order. She spent 15 years making pies for Bill Zuber's Dugout Restaurant in Homestead.

Bakers are early risers. The oven is lit around 2:30 am and

Middle Amana

Doris and Jack Hahn carried on the communal bakery tradition of their family. Come early for the coffee cakes, rolls, and breads. (Photo courtesy of Hahn's Hearth Oven Bakery.)

heats for approximately three hours. The oven is then turned off, and the heated bricks attain the correct temperature to bake the day's bread. Inside, the oven is 10 feet wide and 10 feet deep and holds 140 loaves of bread at a time. About 350 items can be baked in about two hours in the hearth oven.

A wonderful aroma engulfs the bakery's small purchasing area, and shoppers must come early in the morning to get the fullest selection. The bakery offers hard-crusted white, rye, and wheat breads in pan-shaped loaves and small rounds. The white and rye are also available in rounds and vienna loaves. Dinner rolls are available in white, rye, and whole wheat.

For those with a sweet tooth, the bakery has a wide range of coffee cakes including cherry, apricot, raspberry, cinnamon, and apple. Streusel coffee cakes are available in cherry, apricot, raspberry, and apple. Also available are cinnamon rolls, kolaches, and twists.

■ Lakeview Village Retirement Community [11]

Telephone: 319-622-6500

This retirement community offers independent-living townhouses with single-level floor plans featuring two bedrooms, two full bathrooms, laundry facilities, a complete eat-in kitchen, and an attached garage. Also available for rent are assisted-living apartments with kitchen appliances. Snow removal and lawn maintenance are provided, and 24-hour emergency medical assistance is available. Housekeeping and meal service is optional. These modern units overlook the Lily Lake and offer convenient access to all the villages. Call or write PO Box 307, Amana, IA 52203 for information packets.

■ Middle Amana Church [8]

Telephone: 319-622-6155
Sunday services: German 8:30 am, English 10:00 am

Visitors are welcome to the Sunday worship of the Amana Church Society. Members ask that you respect the church, service, and traditions. Men and women enter separate doors and are seated on opposite sides of the church, which was built in 1865. Amana Church Society men wear suits, and women wear traditional attire, including black cap, shawl, and apron. Visitors are not required to dress in this fashion.

Elders preside at the ceremony, leading the hymns and providing the readings. Bibles, song books, and program pamphlets are available so the visitor can follow along with the service. Songs are sung a cappella: there are no musical instruments.

The Church is a denomination of the Christian Church, and the service will be somewhat familiar to many. After an opening hymn, an elder reads from the inspired testimony. This is an account of testimony given many years ago by inspired leaders of the Church. Following the inspired testimony is a prayer and a

The Middle Amana Church, built in 1865, welcomes visitors to Sunday morning service. (Photo by author.)

scripture reading from the Bible. An elder then provides a commentary on the testimony or scripture, and a psalm is read. Another hymn and a closing prayer conclude the service.

For more information see the religious beliefs section under A History of the Amana Colonies in the first chapter.

South Amana

There is a little bit of everything representative of the Amana Colonies in South Amana, and everything seems to come in twos. There are two bed and breakfast facilities, two antique shops, two furniture stores, and two museums. An award-winning winery and a handmade rug store round out this small-town pleasure.

In November of 1856, South Amana became the third village settled. South Amana had been inhabited by earlier settlers who built a few cabins in the area. The Colonists purchased the land primarily to manage the western land holdings of the community. Large herds of cattle, hogs, and sheep were raised nearby. Abundant clay allowed for easy brickmaking, and the structures in South Amana have more brick than the other villages. Nearly every building was built of brick, including chicken coops and hog sheds. Farm buildings were located at one end of the village and shops at the other. In between were the church, seven communal kitchen houses, and residences.

South Amana had a bakery, blacksmith, brickyard, broom shop, butcher shop and smokehouse, carpenter, carpet weaver, cooper or tinsmith, depot, drying house, furniture shop, general store, hotel, ice house, lumber office and feed store, press house, pump house, sawmill, school, tailor, wagon and harness shop, and winery. Agricultural buildings included an apiary, corncrib, elevator, feed mill, grain elevator, grain office, granary, implement shed, milk house, oxen barn, sheep barn, and steer barn.

Upper South Amana, just a few miles south and up the big hill, was developed to serve the Chicago, Milwaukee, St. Paul, and Pacific Railroad Company, which opened a depot in 1883 on the bluff. Today, the town has several homes and the Amana Society Bakery, which, although not open to the public, offers

Amana Colonies Guide

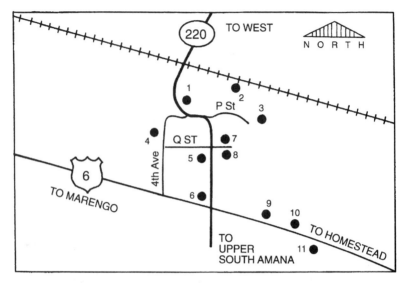

South Amana
1. South Amana Barn Museum
2. Communal Agriculture Museum
3. Former Colony Market Place Restaurant
4. Granary Emporium
5. Ackerman Winery and Cheese Shop
6. Fern Hill Gifts and Quilts
7. Baeckerei Bed and Breakfast
8. Berger's Hand Woven Rugs
9. Schanz Furniture and Refinishing Shop
10. Krauss Furniture and Clock Factory
11. Bábi's Bed and Breakfast

Map numbers also appear beside the description of each establishment.

baked items for purchase throughout the Colonies. Upper South Amana offers a good view of all of the villages. To the east of Upper South is one of the few remaining pine forests which were planted in the villages. Most of the Amana pine forests were cut down to provide lumber during World War II, at the request of the U.S. government.

Lodging Facilities

▪ Bábi's Bed and Breakfast [11]

▪ QUICK FACTS
Telephone: 319-662-4381
Internet address: http://www.jeonet.com/amanas/babis.htm
Number of rooms: eight
Rate range: $59–$89
Payment methods: cash, check, Discover, MasterCard, Visa
Reservations: two-night minimum, deposit required, refundable 14 days prior to stay
Check in: 3:00 pm–7:00 pm
Check out: 10:30 am
Private baths: six with private bath, two with shared bath
Amenities: air-conditioning; handmade bedspreads; spacious grounds with walking trails, gazebo, and swings; no alcohol
Breakfast: continental breakfast including homemade pastries

The gazebo and grounds of the ten-acre Bábi's Bed and Breakfast retreat. (Photo by author.)

Parking: ample parking near rooms
Handicap accessible: yes
Smoking: not in bedrooms
Children: age 12 and older
Pets: no
Farmhouse built: 1906 as a farmhouse
Barn units remodeled: 1991 as an inn
Retreat opened: 1987
Hosts: Marilyn and Tom Kessler

Bábi's Bed and Breakfast offers accommodations in the main house and in a remodeled barn. Bábi's is a secluded, ten-acre retreat featuring wooded paths, a gazebo, and abundant wildlife. Tom fenced off the area many years ago and enjoys his own wildlife preserve. It is not uncommon to see deer, wild turkey, pheasant, squirrels, and rabbits on the grounds.

Bábi is Czechoslovakian for grandmother, and family is an integral part of Tom and Marilyn Kessler's operation. Tom and Marilyn bought the farm in 1965 and raised their four daughters on the spacious grounds. Even though their children have grown up, married, and moved on, they still help with the business. The daughters have helped design brochures, developed a home page on the Internet, and created crafts that hang on the walls in various rooms.

The main house has a large, wrap-around porch which allows a wide-angle view of the grounds. It offers four rooms, each named for one of the four daughters: Shelley, Stacy, Susan, and Sarah. Two of the bedrooms have a queen bed and share a bathroom with tub and shower. The other two rooms are connected and share a bathroom, but one room has a queen bed and the other a twin bed. Marilyn made the bedspreads and tablecloths in the house, and many paintings by their daughter Stacy grace the walls.

The barn has four bedrooms named after the Kesslers' sons-in-law: Merlin, Tom, Mitch, and Mike. Tom remodeled the barn unit into modern hotel rooms. The rooms offer different colors, but all are carpeted and have showers and queen-size beds. Various crafts accent the rooms. "We tried to keep it country and simple," says Marilyn.

In addition to the four bedrooms, a loft runs the length of the top and offers plenty of space and many amenities. The hayloft can sleep four on a queen bed and a fold-out couch. A full tub and shower, a kitchen table and chairs, and a small refrigerator and microwave oven make this a useful room for travelers. The loft is topped off by skylights and a private sundeck which is ideal for enjoying a comfortable evening on the farm. Tom says the loft is the most popular room and should be booked at least a month ahead of time.

Outside the buildings, guests can relax in the yard swing or gazebo or on one of several benches. Tom has added arbors and walking bridges, and he mows the walking trails for easier hiking. A barbecue grill is available, or the Kesslers can arrange for a bonfire complete with a marshmallow and hot dog roast.

All guests can use the first floor of the home where the kitchen and living room are located. The living room contains the only available television, radio, and telephone at the retreat. A piano and guitar are also available.

Breakfast is served at 8:00 am and consists of coffee, orange juice, pastries, breads, fruit cup, jellies, and jams. The pastries are homemade by Marilyn using many old Czech recipes. Homemade cookies are found throughout the day on the kitchen table. The Kesslers also make their own grape jelly and caramel sauce.

■ Baeckerei Bed and Breakfast [7]

■ Quick Facts
Telephone: 319-622-3597/800-391-8650
Number of rooms: three
Rate range: $50 two persons, $10 for third
Payment methods: cash, check, MasterCard, Visa
Reservations: recommended, 48-hour cancellation required
Check-in: 2:00 pm–5:00 pm
Check-out: 11:00 am

The queen-size pencil-post-frame bed at Baeckerei Bed and Breakfast, an old communal bakery. (Photo by author.)

Private baths: yes
Amenities: air-conditioning, color television with cable, king and queen beds, ceiling fans
Breakfast: full breakfast
Parking: in rear
Handicap accessible: no
Smoking: no
Children: over 12
Pets: no
Building: constructed 1864 as a bakery, second-story residence added in 1921
Inn opened: 1991
Hosts: Paula and Wally Pasbrig

When Paula and Wally Pasbrig decided to move to South Amana, Paula wanted an old house and Wally wanted a bed and breakfast. They got both in the Baeckerei Bed and Breakfast.

Bäckerei (a variant of Baeckerei) is German for bakery. The building was originally built in 1864 and was used as the community bakery, supplying bread and other baked goods to the local communal kitchen houses. The bakery's hearth oven is still intact, and Wally has remodeled the home around the old-style oven.

Three upstairs rooms, each connected to a common parlor area, are available for guests. One room has a king-size bed and a bathroom with shower. A second room has a queen-size bed with a pencil-post frame and a love seat that converts into a bed. The third room is the Christmas Room; it has a queen-size bed and a bathroom with shower. As one might expect from its name, this room is decorated in a Christmas motif, including Santa Claus decorations. All of the rooms have wooden floors, a wardrobe, coordinating rugs, ceiling fans, cable television, and cross-stitch decorations which Wally created himself. Portable phones are also available.

The Pasbrigs will interact with guests only as much as the guests prefer. "We're here to help answer questions, refer restaurants, and to get things like ice," says Wally. "And we encourage guests to have a good time and enjoy their stay," he adds.

A big breakfast is served in the dining room at 8:30 am and includes your choice of cereal, scrambled eggs, or a special such as quiche lorraine or stuffed French toast strata. The stuffed French toast strata is French-bread cubes, cream cheese, eggs, and sauce, baked golden brown and served with an apple cider syrup. All breakfast choices are served with juice, fruit cup, meat, toast, jelly, and coffee. "We like to have guests leave breakfast full," says Wally.

Paula selects the wallpaper, rugs, and other decorations, and Wally installs it all. Wally has been busy finishing the family's living quarters with the help of their two boys. One of the boys does the matting and framing for most of the art work in the house.

Paula and Wally purchased the home in 1989 and opened their bed and breakfast in 1991. In addition to the family living quarters, the downstairs houses the guest dining room and a gift shop which stocks an abundance of items such as wood crafts, paintings, and Christmas items, many handcrafted by Paula and her mother.

SHOPS AND TOURIST ATTRACTIONS

■ Ackerman Winery and Cheese Shop [5]

Telephone: 319-622-3379
Fax: 319-622-6513
Hours: Mon–Sat 9:00 am–6:00 pm, Sun 10:00 am–5:00 pm

The wine and cheese shops are located in a former communal kitchen, residence, woodshed, and washhouse built in 1867. Ackermans have over 12,000 gallons of hand-bottled wine in storage. Several award-winning wines are for sale, as are 20 wine varieties such as black raspberry, Catawba grape, dandelion, Riesling, and White Zinfandel. Among the more unusual wines available are red clover, black currant, and honey wines. The cheese shop offers 30 cheese varieties as well as jellies, crackers, sausages, and gifts. Shoppers can sample wines and cheeses. Both stores have gift items including food, throw rugs, baskets, and chimes.

Wines from the Ackerman Winery and Cheese Shop have won several awards. (Photo by author.)

■ Berger's Hand Woven Rugs [8]

Telephone: 319-622-3174
Hours: variable, so knock at the adjacent house for service

Berger's offers handwoven rugs in a variety of patterns and colors. Materials used include cotton, cotton blends, wool, and denim from recycled blue jeans. The rugs are located in an old cabinet shop which features an assortment of old tools as well as the two 60-year-old looms which are used to produce the rugs. Custom orders are welcome, or visitors can choose from rugs three to six feet long, in widths of 28 and 36 inches, which are shown in the shop.

George Berger, who makes the rugs, is a third-generation craftsman. His father and grandfather did cabinetwork, and his mother and her father made rugs. George did the carpeting for the Herbert Hoover presidential birthplace in West Branch, Iowa. If the shop looks closed, follow the sidewalk to the house for assistance.

The building housing the rug shop was built in 1865 as a cooper and broom shop. The residence was built in 1869.

■ Communal Agriculture Museum [2]

Telephone: 319-622-3567
Hours: May 1–Sep 30, Mon–Sat 10:00 am–5:00 pm, Sun 12:00 pm–5:00 pm

The Communal Agriculture Museum is housed in an old ox barn built around 1860; it offers a glimpse of how Amana farm workers utilized various tools to work the land. With 16,000 farm acres and 10,000 acres of timber, much work needed to be done. On display is equipment which was used for planting, plowing, harvesting, hay making, road grading, livestock management, ice harvesting, blacksmithing, and harness and wagon making.

Ice was harvested and stored in buildings with sawdust to provide year-round ice for meals. Homestead ice pond, circa 1910. (Photo courtesy Amana Heritage Society.)

There was no private property under the communal system because all land and buildings were owned by the Community. For purposes of management, cropland, pasture, and timber were divided among the seven villages, and the village farm boss managed the operation, including assigning workers to handle the various chores such as working with hogs, cattle, dairy cattle, sheep, and horses.

Today, the Amana Society manages the farm operations, which consist of corn, soybean, and sorghum harvesting and a beef cattle operation.

Admission is $1 for adults and 50 cents for children over eight. A combination ticket to all four of the Amana Heritage Society Museums is available.

■ Fern Hill Gifts and Quilts [6]

Telephone: 319-622-3627
Hours: Mon–Sat 9:30 am–5:00 pm, Sun 12:00 pm–5:00 pm

Originally built in the 1880s as a general store and residence, Fern Hill offers an abundance of antiques and quilts, and many food items in its tearoom. The store is jam-packed with dried and everlasting flowers, quilts and quilt supplies, porcelain dolls, teddy bears, folk art, hand carvings, candles, furniture, and Hoffman fabrics. The tearoom features various sandwiches, pastries, fudge, ice cream, and gourmet coffee and tea.

In 1877, Jesse James and his gang robbed the store and tied up the clerks, Emil Wolf and Charles Ratzel, who lived in the second-floor residence. The building burned in 1885 and was rebuilt. A sandwich shop opened here in 1938. The building became a general store and later a gift shop, until Fern Hill opened in 1990.

■ Granary Emporium [4]

Telephone: 319-622-3195
Hours: daily 10:00 am–5:00 pm

The Granary is a two-story antique store with a little of everything, including creaky wood floors. The building, constructed in 1865 and used for grain storage, now offers gifts, furniture, glassware, collectibles, and crafts. This rare brick granary features the only arched doorway in the Colonies. The building was purchased and restored in 1985. It is the only brick granary in the seven villages.

■ Krauss Furniture and Clock Factory [10]

Telephone: 319-622-3223
Hours: Mon–Fri 8:00 am–5:00 pm, Sat 9:00 am–5:00 pm, May–Dec Sun 1:00 pm–4:00 pm

Krauss Furniture offers a short, self-guided tour of the factory, where you can see the craftsmanship they invest in their solid walnut, oak, and cherry pieces. A huge selection of clocks highlights the store, which offers mantle, carriage, wall, grandfather, grandmother, and granddaughter clocks. Krauss also sells chairs, tables, dressers, curio cabinets, bookcases, hutches, buffets, nightstands, coffee tables, mirrors, quilt stands, and oak cradles. Krauss offers many Queen Anne and Mission style pieces.

Handmade items line the store, and custom-built pieces from any wood can be designed from photographs or sketches.

■ Schanz Furniture and Refinishing Shop [9]

Telephone: 319-622-3529
Hours: Mon–Sat 8:00 am–5:00 pm

Schanz Furniture offers hundreds of furniture pieces featuring solid walnut, oak, and cherry woods, and they will custom make any item from any wood. They offer furniture restoration, repairing, and refinishing as well as caning and seat weaving. Schanz makes furniture in the old Amana way with mortise and tenon construction, panel sides, and dovetail drawers without center guides.

Browsing through the store, one finds rockers, stools, benches, cabinets, dressers, beds, chests, nightstands, desks, hutches, chairs, tables, tea carts, bookcases, buggy benches, and wooden toys.

■ South Amana Barn Museum [1]

Telephone: 319-622-3058
Hours: daily 9:00 am–5:00pm, Apr–Oct
Admission: $3.50 adults, children depending on age

This is a privately operated museum featuring the miniature works of Henry Moore. Moore spent years creating his version of rural America, with hundreds of miniature replicas including his Amana reproductions, a pioneer Iowa farmstead, small-town

Americana, Abraham Lincoln's village of New Salem, Illinois, an 1890s California logging camp, a Native American village, the Little Brown Church, and an 1840s Louisiana sugar plantation.

Moore went to great lengths to create his work of art. For instance, the Amana granary has 2,290 pieces of wood and 200 screws, and an Amana barn uses 9,897 nails in drilled holes. Moore built his first piece in 1968, scaled one inch to the foot.

The museum is housed in an old horse barn, which burned when struck by lightning in 1913, killing all 22 horses housed there. The barn was subsequently rebuilt.

Amana Colonies Guide

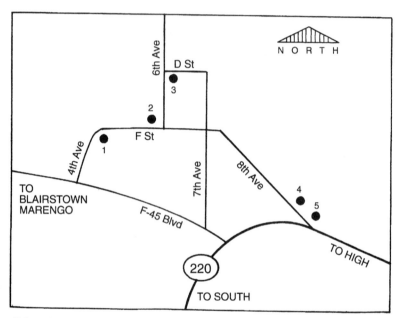

West Amana
1. Corner House Bed and Breakfast
2. West Amana General Store
3. Cricket on the Hearth Antiques
4. Schanz Furniture and Gift Shop
5. Broom and Basket Shop

Map numbers also appear beside the description of each establishment.

West Amana

West Amana is a quiet and peaceful hillside community. It offers a bed and breakfast, two antique shops, a furniture showroom, and a broom and basket shop.

As the second Amana village, West Amana was established in October 1856, just a month before South Amana, which was established in November. A few log huts existed in the spot where the village was to be settled, so residents of Amana traveled daily to West Amana to dismantle, move, and rebuild the huts into the first house. Next, they constructed a horse barn and kitchen house. At this point, the colonists were able to stay permanently in West Amana and begin work on the other essential village buildings and homes.

Farm buildings were located at one end of the village and shops at the other. In between were a church, seven communal kitchen houses, and communal residences.

Shops and buildings in the village included an ash house, bakery, basket shop, blacksmith, butcher shop, carpenter, drying houses, flour mill, garden house, general store, harness shop, hobo shack, ice house, locksmith, lumber shed, press house, sawmill, school, shoemaker, tank house, and wagon shop. In addition, the village had orchards and a sandstone quarry.

Agricultural buildings included apiaries, a cow barn, a bull and calf barn, a foal barn, hog barns, a horned-cattle barn, a horse barn, a farm implement building, a granary, an oxen barn, a sheep barn, and a shed for a stationary threshing machine.

Lodging Facilities

■ Corner House Bed and Breakfast [1]*

■ Quick Facts
Telephone: 319-622-6390/800-996-6964
Number of rooms: four, with more planned
Rate range: $35–$45
Payment methods: cash, check, MasterCard, Visa
Reservations: recommended, 48-hour notice of cancellation required for full refund
Check-in: 1:00 pm
Check-out: 11:00 am
Private baths: yes
Amenities: air-conditioning, cable television, refrigerator in rooms
Breakfast: full breakfast
Parking: in front
Handicap accessible: downstairs bedroom accessible, short steps required to enter building
Smoking: no
Children: yes
Pets: no
Building: constructed around 1862 as a communal residence
Inn opened: 1996
Hosts: David and Yana Cutler

The Corner House in West Amana is one of the newest inns in the Colonies. The proprietors are David and Yana Cutler. David is from Idaho and Yana from Czechoslovakia. When the couple moved to Iowa for David's new job, they stayed at Rawson's Bed and Breakfast in Homestead, where they fell in love with the bed and breakfast concept. They went looking for a house and found one on the corner of a hillside road in West Amana.

The stone portion of the inn was originally built in 1862 as a granary but was soon converted to a residence. After the Great Change of 1932, the building became a residential home for three

---
* The number refers to location on the village map.

The Corner House is the latest bed and breakfast addition to the Colonies. (Photo courtesy of Corner House.)

The mahogany frame queen bed at the Corner House Bed and Breakfast. (Photo courtesy of Corner House).

families. The Cutlers moved into the home in January 1996 and immediately began renovations for the bed and breakfast. It has four rooms available, with plans for additional rooms as David and Yana continue to remodel. Yana calls her rooms the Doily Room, the Candle Room, the Amana Blue Room, and Grandma's Quilt Room.

Many antiques appear throughout the sandstone house, and the inn shows the influence of Yana'a heritage in its European wallpaper and in the Czechoslovakian decorative eggs and cookies that hang on the walls. Yana also did the stenciling work in the house.

On the ground floor are the Doily Room and the sitting or living room. The Doily Room features a mahogany queen bed and dresser, carpeting, a television, a small refrigerator, a full-length mirror, and a bathroom with a shower and a whirlpool bath. Fresh flowers decorate the room, and little touches such as petals in the toilet make the Doily Room special for guests. The sitting room offers a comfortable stop where the traveler can relax and unwind. The floor is covered with a Persian rug, and the room has a wood-burning fireplace, ceiling fan, love seat, rocker, and chairs.

Upstairs are the Pine Room, where breakfast is served, and the other three guest rooms. On the stairway up to the Pine Room, Amana baskets and quilts are featured. The Pine Room is furnished with a Chinese rug which covers the wooden floor, an Amana couch, chairs, and a big table for enjoying Yana's special morning meal. Breakfast includes fresh fruit in season, home-baked muffins, rolls, kolaches or crepes, omelets, Amana ham or sausage platters, coffee, tea, juice, and milk. Sometimes Yana prepares morning casseroles.

The three upstairs guest rooms all have cable television, air-conditioning, small refrigerators, European-style bathrooms with sinks on the outside of the bathroom, and Yana's stenciling touches. The Candle Room has a queen bed, full bath, dresser, and mirror. The bedroom is decorated in a light vanilla color with lace curtains, hand-stenciled borders, a floral quilt, and hanging candles. The Amana Blue Room and Grandma's Quilt Room are similar to one another. Each room has twin beds with a table, chairs, and a rocker. Each room has lace curtains, and Yana's stenciling flows around the sloped ceilings. Each bathroom has a shower unit.

Also upstairs is a small library area with a rocker and an Amana couch. Original paintings of Prague, the capital of the Czech Republic, hang on the walls, and there is a variety of reading material on the shelves and tables.

Original Amana-style locks are on all the doors. Rollaway beds are available, and gift certificates are offered.

SHOPS AND TOURIST ATTRACTIONS

■ Broom and Basket Shop [5]

Telephone: 319-622-3315
Hours: Mon–Sat 9:00 am–5:00 pm (cut back in winter); Sun 12:00 pm–5:00 pm, Jun–Aug only

The Broom and Basket Shop offers brooms in all shapes and sizes, each with a different purpose. The store also has a tremendous selection of baskets, most made locally by talented basket makers. Owner Joanna Schanz helped revive the basket industry in the Colonies. She can sometimes be found weaving baskets at the Amana Arts Guild in West Amana.

The meticulous work of a master broom maker, Jacob Morbach, circa 1920s. (Photo courtesy Amana Heritage Society.)

■ Cricket on the Hearth Antiques [3]

Telephone: 319-622-3088
Hours: Wed–Sun 10:00 am–5:00 pm, May–Oct

This antique store offers unique, quality gifts on two levels. The cricket on hearth is a good luck charm, derived from Chinese history, as well as from the Charles Dickens story. The building was constructed in 1869 as a communal kitchen house and residence. The owners have worked to restore the home and grounds to their pre-1932 condition.

The Cricket on the Hearth antique shop was an 1869 communal kitchen house. (Photo by author.)

■ Schanz Furniture and Gift Shop [4]

Telephone: 319-622-3315
Hours: Mon–Sat 9:00 am–5:00 pm (cut back in winter); Sun 12:00 pm–5:00 pm, Jun–Aug only

Schanz's main furniture shop is located in South Amana, but you can find the same furniture at this outlet store, which is next to the Broom and Basket Shop. "Windmill Willy" stands out front, and Iowa's largest solid walnut rocker is on display inside. It contains over 300 board feet of walnut, weighs 670 pounds, and took over 130 hours to build, finish, and cane at a cost of $3,000.

■ West Amana General Store [2]

Telephone: 319-622-3945
Hours: daily 10:00 am–5:00 pm

The West Amana General Store was built to handle supplies for the communal kitchens in West Amana and to allow villagers to obtain various individual items needed in their homes. Today, visitors will find many antiques and gift items in the 5,000-square-foot store. There are antiques on three levels, and a little bit of everything is featured. The store was built in 1862, and the concrete block addition to the north was added in 1913.

Little Amana Interstate Complex and Vicinity

Little Amana is not one of the seven villages. It was developed along Interstate 80 to offer a touch of the Amanas to travelers, giving them a place to eat, sleep, and shop.

At Little Amana, visitors will find a tourism welcome center with handmade gift items, three restaurants, a large Holiday Inn complex, four other hotels, a bed and breakfast, a gas station, and a series of Amana Society businesses offering woolen products, wine, food items, and various gifts. Five miles to the west, at I-80 exit 220, is the 65-store Tanger Outlet Center, several restaurants and fast-food shops, and more lodging facilities. Four miles further west, at I-80 exit 216, is a rural bed and breakfast which offers a farm tour and gourmet breakfasts.

From the Little Amana interstate complex, visitors can join the Amana Colonies Trail, a highway system which leads through each of the seven villages.

The Little Amana complex, located on Interstate 80, offers Amana products, food, and overnight accommodations. (Photo by author.)

Amana Colonies Guide

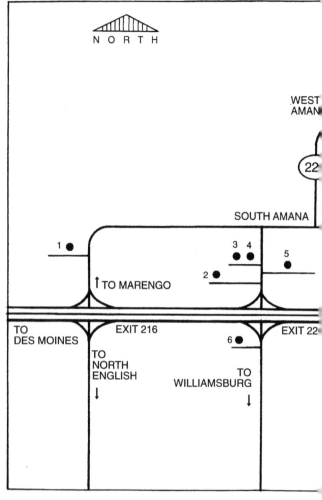

Little Amana Interstate Complex
1. Loy's Bed and Breakfast
2. Crest Motel
3. Super 8, exit 220
4. Best Western Quiet House Suites
5. Tanger Outlet Center (shopping mall)
6. Ramada Limited
7. Comfort Inn
8. Little Amana Woolen Outlet
9. Little Amana General Store
10. Little Amana Winery

Little Amana Interstate Complex

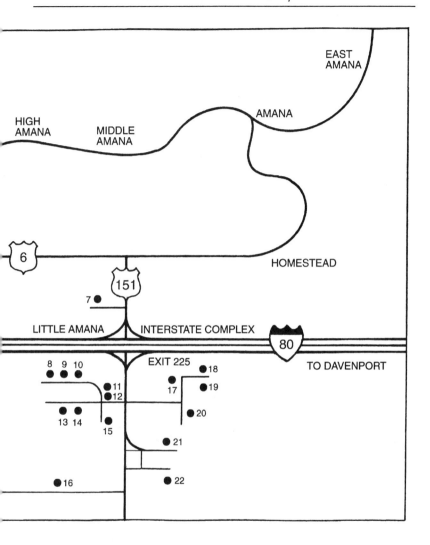

11. Iowa Welcome Center
12. Flora 'n Fauna: Etc.
13. Amana Holiday Inn
14. Seven Villages Restaurant
15. Little Amana HandiMart
16. Lucille's Bett und Breakfast
17. Colony Haus Restaurant
18. My Little Inn
19. Day's Inn
20. Fetzer's Standard
21. Colony Village Restaurant
22. Super 8, exit 225

Map numbers also appear beside the description of each establishment.

Restaurants

■ Colony Haus Restaurant [17]*

■ QUICK FACTS
Telephone: 319-668-1443
Hours: daily 6:00 am–10:00 pm
Capacity: 400
Groups: yes
Parking: large lot, bus parking available
Handicap accessible: yes
Smoking: in designated areas only
Price range: breakfast $6.75, lunch $4.50–$6.95, dinner $9.50–$13.50
Payment methods: cash, check, American Express, Discover, MasterCard, Visa
Family-style dining: yes
Children's menu: yes
Customer favorites: coleslaw, jumbo cinnamon rolls, Saturday prime rib, German chocolate pie
Building: constructed 1967 as a restaurant
Restaurant opened: 1967
Hosts: Gerry and Fay Schuerer

The Colony Haus building housed the first restaurant to operate at the Little Amana complex. The original restaurant was called the Colony Village Restaurant. The name was changed to Colony Haus in 1976, when Gerry and Fay Schuerer, of Amana, began operating the restaurant.

Gerry's parents, Walt and Florence, operate the Brick Haus restaurant in Amana, and Gerry has been in the restaurant business for a number of years, both with his family's operation in Amana and with the Bishops restaurant chain.

The Colony Haus offers the All American Platter, a house specialty featuring smoked pork chop, *Wiener Schnitzel* (breaded veal cutlet), and sausage. The restaurant also features specials: catfish on Friday night; prime rib on Saturday night; and a

---
* The number refers to location on the village map.

House Feast, featuring three meats in an all-you-can-eat sitting, on Sunday.

While the menu features the traditional German fare found in many of the village restaurants, Gerry says the interstate traffic has led him to offer many short-order items, including several sandwich choices. The Colony Haus uses only cholesterol-free oil for frying.

The coffee shop, with tables, booths, and a counter, is a casual area to enjoy breakfast, lunch, or dinner. The main dining rooms can be connected or separated for banquets, parties, or small-group dining. A carpeted, full-service lounge area is decorated with wildlife prints. A gift area features souvenirs and food items such as candy, beer, breads, and wine.

■ MENU SAMPLE

Appetizers: breaded mushrooms, onion straws, and breaded dill pickles.

Breakfast: family-style breakfast includes orange juice, scrambled eggs, hash browns, bacon, sausage, pancake and syrup, fruit bowl, homemade preserves, toast, and beverage; also available are omelets, steak and eggs, cinnamon rolls, oatmeal, dry cereal, blueberry or strawberry pancakes, French toast, and Belgian waffles.

Lunch: chicken, shrimp, fish, turkey, chicken pot pie, beef and noodles, chicken and broccoli pasta alfredo, and chicken marinara; pork tenderloin, reuben, hot roast beef, French dip, and grilled ham and cheese sandwiches; stuffed tomato and croissant; soups; and chef's, grilled chicken, Caesar, chicken walnut, seafood, and tuna salads.

Family-style dining: includes refillable bowls of coleslaw, cottage cheese, salad, potatoes, gravy, vegetable, sauerkraut, and bread and butter.

Dinner items: fried chicken, Amana smoked pork chop, Amana pork sausage, *Sauerbraten* (marinated beef), *Weiner Schnitzel* (breaded veal cutlet), Swiss steak, sirloin steak, New York strip, prime rib, steak and shrimp, scallops, whitefish, and catfish.

Light eaters: chicken, shrimp, or fish baskets; ground sirloin; turkey breasts; chef's, chicken, or seafood salads; and fruit plate.

Sandwiches: pork tenderloin, ham, reuben, chicken filet, French dip, ham and cheese, Amana grilled sausage, Amana bratwurst, and fish.

Children's menu: chicken strips with French fries and beverage, or hamburger, grilled cheese, hot dog, and family dinners at reduced prices.

Desserts: homemade pies including German chocolate, apple, cherry, red raspberry, and rhubarb; strawberry shortcake, sundaes; ice cream; and sherbet.

Beverages: coffee, tea, iced tea, milk, soft drinks, lemonade, chocolate milk, and hot chocolate.

Alcoholic beverages: domestic and imported beer including Amana Millstream and Heineken; cocktails; Amana wines; and Paul Masson wines.

■ Colony Village Restaurant [21]

■ QUICK FACTS
Telephone: 319-668-1223
Hours: daily 6:00 am–10:00 pm
Capacity: 450
Groups: yes
Parking: large lot, bus parking available
Handicap accessible: yes
Smoking: in designated areas only
Price range: breakfast $7, lunch $4.50–$7, dinner $9.25–$11.95
Payment methods: cash, American Express, Carte Blanche, Diner's Club, Discover, MasterCard, Visa
Family-style dining: yes
Children's menu: yes
Customer favorites: breakfast special, family-style breakfast, Village Banquet
Building: constructed 1976 as a restaurant
Restaurant opened: 1976
Hosts: Russ and Bob Sandersfield

Little Amana Interstate Complex

Russ and Bob Sandersfield have operated a restaurant at the Little Amana complex since 1967, when they opened the Colony Village Restaurant in the building which now houses the Colony Haus Restaurant.

In 1976, Russ and Bob built a new building on the hill and kept the Colony Village name. The large restaurant has a coffee shop, meeting room, gift shop, lounge, and large dining rooms. The coffee shop has booths and counters in a country setting with early-Amana photographs. The meeting room can handle sizable groups. The gift shop features souvenirs, books, stuffed animals, Iowa Hawkeye items, and local food products such as breads, beer, and wine. The spacious lounge has two levels with many tables and a big-screen television. The main floor dining rooms are large rooms which can be partitioned for banquets and parties. A lower-level dining room is also available.

At breakfast, a popular order is a special with two eggs, bacon, two pancakes or toast, and beverage. Breakfast lovers also enjoy the Village's family-style breakfast with its all-you-can-eat items. For dinner, the popular Village Banquet features three meat entrees served with refillable bowls of food in the family-style dining tradition.

■ Menu Sample

Appetizers: shrimp cocktail, onion rings, and pickled Amana ham.

Breakfast: family-style breakfast includes two or three meats (bacon, ham, sausage) with eggs, fried potatoes, toast, juice, and coffee; also available are a breakfast special, blueberry pancakes, buttermilk pancakes, French toast, Belgian malted waffles, omelets, fruit, rolls, and tomato, grapefruit, prune, and orange juice.

Lunch: sandwiches are served with French fries and coleslaw and include German bratwurst, *Wiener Schnitzel* (breaded veal cutlet), reuben, chicken breast, fish, pork tenderloin, hamburger, cheeseburger, bacon-lettuce-tomato, baked Amana ham, ham and cheese, grilled cheese, and roast beef.

Family-style dinners: include refillable bowls of potatoes, gravy, vegetable, coleslaw, cottage cheese, and bread and butter.

Dinner items: *Wiener Schnitzel* (breaded veal cutlet), *Sauerbraten* (marinated beef), *Kassler Rippchen* (smoked pork chops), Iowa pork chop, Amana bratwurst, Amana ham steak, Amana sausage, fried chicken, beef tenderloin, T-bone steak, ribeye steak, top sirloin steak, oven-baked steak, ground sirloin, lobster, scallops, catfish, breaded shrimp, breaded fish filet, Canadian walleye pike, steak and shrimp, and steak and lobster.
Children's menu: hamburger, chicken drumstick, chicken strips, and hot dogs.
Desserts: a variety of pies, strawberry shortcake, sundaes, ice cream, and sherbet.
Beverages: coffee, tea, iced tea, whole or skim milk, buttermilk, chocolate milk, soft drinks, and lemonade.
Alcoholic beverages: domestic and imported beer on tap and in bottles, including Amana Millstream, Heineken, DAB, and St. Pauli Girl; cocktails; champagne; sherry; Amana Colony wines; and Gallo, Christian Brothers, and Ingelnook wines.

■ Seven Villages Restaurant [14]

■ QUICK FACTS
Telephone: 319-668-2157
Hours: coffee shop 6:00 am–10:00 pm daily; dining room Mon–Thu 5:00 pm–9:00 pm, Fri–Sat 5:00 pm–10:00 pm, Sun 11:00 am–9:00 pm
Capacity: coffee shop 120, dining room 120
Groups: yes
Parking: ample parking in front and on side
Handicap accessible: yes
Smoking: in designated areas of dining room only
Price range: coffee shop lunch $2.25–$7.50, dinner $8.95–$14.95
Payment methods: cash, check, American Express, Discover, MasterCard, Visa
Family-style dining: yes, in dining room
Children's menu: yes
Customer favorites: family-style breakfast, large omelets and homemade cinnamon rolls in the coffee shop; Harvestfest dinner in the dining room
Building: constructed 1971 as a restaurant

Little Amana Interstate Complex

Restaurant opened: 1971
Hosts: managed by Triangle Management for the Amana Nordstrom Company

The Seven Villages Restaurant is connected to the Amana Holiday Inn. The restaurant has a large coffee shop and a dining room which serve hotel guests and many travelers. The Village Pump Lounge, located between the restaurant and the hotel, features appetizers and a full-service bar in an inviting setting.

The coffee shop is carpeted and has tables and booths, photographs of the early Colonies, and antique tool decorations. The main dining room has a country theme, is also carpeted, and consists of tables and buggy booths, which resemble old, horse-drawn buggies.

Breakfast is popular in the coffee shop and features giant homemade cinnamon rolls and large omelets. The Seven Villages Restaurant also serves a family-style breakfast with all-you-can-eat items. Popular items in the dining room include the *Sauerbraten* (marinated beef); *Wiener Schnitzel* (breaded veal cutlet); and the Harvestfest, which features three meats and family-style dining.

■ Menu Sample

Appetizers: pickled ham, mozzarella sticks, buffalo wings, onion rings, and buffalo shrimp.

Breakfast: large omelets, homemade cinnamon rolls, and family-style, all-you-can-eat breakfasts.

Family-style dining: the Harvestfest features three meats, three salads, bread and butter, potatoes, gravy, vegetable, sauerkraut, and homemade dessert.

Dinner items: *Wiener Schnitzel* (breaded veal cutlet), *Sauerbraten* (marinated beef), *Kassler Rippchen* (smoked pork chops), Amana bratwurst, fried chicken, hickory-smoked ham steak, oven-baked steak, baby beef liver, grilled chicken breasts, T-bone steak, beef tenderloin, top sirloin, prime rib, prime rib and shrimp, prime rib and chicken, deep-fried jumbo shrimp, cod, shrimp and scallops, catfish on Fridays, and homemade giblet dressing and homestyle noodles on Sunday.

Coffee shop: appetizers; soups; salads; and sandwiches, including reubens, pork tenderloins, Amana bratwurst, burgers, chicken, and bacon-lettuce-tomato.

Children's menu in the dining room: chicken; ham; oven-baked steak; fish; shrimp; and hamburger, fries, and soft drink.

Children's menu in the coffee shop: grilled cheese sandwich, hot dogs, peanut butter and jelly sandwich, chicken planks, hot beef sandwich, and ham dinner with gelatin.

Desserts: pies such as rhubarb, cherry, raisin cream, peach, and chocolate or coconut cream; apple cobbler; chocolate brownie sundae; German chocolate cheesecake; ice cream; and milkshakes.

Beverages: coffee, tea, iced tea, two percent milk, skim milk, chocolate milk, buttermilk, and soft drinks.

Alcoholic beverages: draft and bottled domestic, imported, and nonalcoholic beers including Beck's, Dortmunder, Heineken, DAB, and Amana Millstream; domestic wines.

LODGING FACILITIES, EXIT 225

■ Amana Holiday Inn   [13]

■ QUICK FACTS
Telephone: 319-668-1175/800-633-9244
Location: I-80 exit 225 South
Number of rooms: 155
Rate range: $60–$90
Payment methods: cash, check, American Express, Diner's Club, Discover, MasterCard, Visa
Reservations: well in advance recommended, cancel by 6:00 pm for refund
Check-in: 3:00 pm
Check-out: 11:00 am
Pets: yes
Smoking: allowed in one building of rooms

Amenities: air-conditioning, cable television, indoor pool, whirlpool, sauna, game room with pool table and ping pong, exercise room, adjacent playground area, Seven Villages Restaurant connected to hotel
Year built: 1971

■ Comfort Inn [7]

■ QUICK FACTS
Telephone: 319-668-2700
Location: I-80 exit 225 North
Number of rooms: 61
Rate range: $68–$115
Payment methods: cash, check, American Express, Diner's Club, MasterCard, Visa
Reservations: recommended, cancel before 6:00 pm for refund
Check-in: 1:00 pm
Check-out: 11:00 am
Pets: allowed in smoking rooms only
Smoking: in designated rooms only
Amenities: air-conditioning, satellite television with HBO, ESPN 1, ESPN 2, continental breakfast, indoor pool, hot tub
Year built: 1996

■ Day's Inn [19]

■ QUICK FACTS
Telephone: 319-668-2097/800-329-7466/fax 319-668-2097
Location: I-80 exit 225 South
Number of rooms: 119
Rate range: $48–$62
Payment methods: cash, check, MasterCard, Visa
Reservations: recommended, 24-hour notice of cancellation
Check-in: 3:00 pm
Check-out: 11:00 am
Pets: yes

Smoking: in designated rooms only
Amenities: air-conditioning, remote cable with HBO and Disney, indoor pool, whirlpool, sauna, complimentary continental breakfast, free local calls, coin laundry, putting green and shuffleboard, fax and copying service, VCR rentals and movies, meeting rooms
Year built: around 1965

■ Lucille's Bett und Breakfast   [16]

■ QUICK FACTS
Telephone: 319-668-1185
Location: I-80 exit 225 South on gravel, two miles west, follow signs
Number of rooms: two
Rate range: $50–$60
Payment methods: cash, check
Reservations: recommended, 48-hour notice required for refund
Check in: flexible
Check out: flexible
Private baths: both rooms share same bath
Amenities: air-conditioning, fireplace, grill, piano, organ, games, fresh flowers
Breakfast: full country-style breakfast with eggs, sausage, potatoes, homemade bread, *Apfelkuchen* (a pastry), kolaches, jams, jellies, coffee, and juice
Parking: in front
Handicap accessible: no
Smoking: no
Children: yes, cribs available
Pets: no
Building: English Tudor home built 1978
Inn opened: 1986
Hosts: Dale and Lucille Bell

■ My Little Inn   [18]

■ QUICK FACTS
Telephone: 319-668-9667

Little Amana Interstate Complex

Location: I-80 Exit 225 South, behind Colony Haus Restaurant
Number of rooms: four
Rate range: $38–$45
Payment methods: cash, check, MasterCard, Visa
Reservations: not necessary
Check-in: flexible
Check-out: 10:00 am–12:00 pm
Pets: no
Smoking: no
Amenities: air-conditioning, color television, refrigerator, microwave
Year built: 1970s

■ Super 8   [22]

■ QUICK FACTS
Telephone: 319-668-2800
Location: I-80 exit 225 South
Number of rooms: 63
Rate range: $38–$44
Payment methods: cash, check, American Express, Discover, MasterCard, Visa
Reservations: cancel by 6:00 pm
Check-in: 2:00 pm
Check-out: 11:00 am
Pets: in smoking rooms only
Smoking: in designated rooms only
Amenities: air-conditioning, remote control satellite television, movie rentals, continental breakfast
Year built: 1985

LODGING FACILITIES, EXIT 220

■ Best Western Quiet House Suites   [4]

■ QUICK FACTS
Telephone: 319-668-9777

Location: I-80 exit 220 North
Number of rooms: 33
Rate range: $83–$145
Payment methods: cash, MasterCard, Visa
Reservations: recommended
Check-in: 2:00 pm
Check-out: 11:00 am
Pets: yes
Smoking: in designated rooms only
Amenities: air-conditioning, cable television, continental breakfast, indoor/outdoor pool
Year built: 1994

■ Crest Motel [2]

■ QUICK FACTS
Telephone: 319-668-1522
Location: I-80 exit 220 North
Number of rooms: 30
Rate range: $32–$55
Payment methods: cash, American Express, Discover, MasterCard, Visa
Reservations: cancel by 6:00 pm for refund
Check-in: flexible
Check-out: 11:00 am
Pets: dogs and cats only
Smoking: in designated rooms only
Amenities: color television with satellite
Year built: 20 rooms in 1969, 10 rooms in 1984

■ Ramada Limited [6]

■ QUICK FACTS
Telephone: 319-668-1000
Location: I-80 exit 220 South
Number of rooms: 40
Rate range: $40–$75

Payment methods: cash, American Express, Diner's Club, MasterCard, Visa
Reservations: recommended, cancel by 6:00 pm for refund
Check-in: after 1:00 pm
Check-out: 11:00 am
Pets: no
Smoking: in designated rooms only
Amenities: air-conditioning, color cable television, exercise room
Year built: remodeled by Ramada in 1994

■ Super 8 [3]

■ QUICK FACTS
Telephone: 319-668-9718
Location: I-80 exit 220 North
Number of rooms: 20
Rate range: $50–$80
Payment methods: cash, American Express, Discover, MasterCard, Visa
Reservations: recommended
Check-in: 2:00 pm
Check-out: 11:00 am
Pets: yes
Smoking: in designated rooms only
Amenities: air-conditioning, color cable television
Year built: 1994

LODGING FACILITIES, EXIT 216

■ Loy's Bed and Breakfast [1]

■ QUICK FACTS
Telephone: 319-642-7787
Location: I-80 exit 216 north one mile, west one to two miles on KK Avenue
Number of rooms: three

Rate range: $45–$55
Payment methods: cash, check
Reservations: recommended, deposit required, one week cancellation for refund
Check-in: flexible
Check-out: flexible
Private bath: one private, one shared
Amenities: air-conditioning, television, fireplace, recreation room with pool table, table tennis, shuffleboard, table games, swing set, sandbox, horseshoes, farm tour, hunting
Breakfast: gourmet breakfast with group choice of 14 different entrees such as sausage and cornmeal waffles, casseroles, and various egg dishes
Parking: in front
Handicap accessible: no
Smoking: no
Children: yes
Pets: no
Building: constructed as a 1976 farmhouse
Inn opened: 1985
Hosts: Robert and Loy Walker

Shops and Tourist Attractions

■ Fetzer's Standard [20]

Telephone: 319-668-1190
Hours: Mon–Fri 6:30 am–12:30 am, Sat–Sun open 24 hours

This station has automobile fuel and a food shop and offers standard convenience-store items.

■ Flora 'n Fauna: Etc. [12]

Telephone: 319-668-9682
Hours: Sun–Thu 9:00 am–5:00 pm, Fri–Sat 8:00 am–6:00 pm

Little Amana Interstate Complex

Located inside the Iowa Welcome Center, Flora 'n Fauna is a gift and craft shop featuring many handmade items, most by local artists.

■ Iowa Welcome Center [11]

Telephone: contact the Amana Colonies Visitors Center in Amana for information
Hours: Sun–Thu 9:00 am–5:00 pm, Fri–Sat 8:00 am–6:00 pm

The Iowa Welcome Center gives visitors tourism information on places and attractions within the state of Iowa, including the Amana Colonies. The Center shows a 10-minute videotape featuring the Amana Colonies.

■ Little Amana General Store [9]

Telephone: 319-668-2744
Hours: Sun–Thu 8:30 am–8:00 pm, Fri–Sat 8:30 am–9:00 pm; closed Christmas Day

The General Store offers an array of gift and food items including local breads, meats, jams, jellies, beer, and wine, as well as cheeses, candy, cookies, and various sundries. Also available are kitchen utensils, toys, books, candles, souvenirs, and collectibles including Hummels, Anri wood carvings, Snowbabies, and Jan Hagara items.

■ Little Amana HandiMart [15]

Telephone: 319-668-2868
Hours: daily 7:00 am–10:00 pm

Fuel, grocery items, snacks, sundries, and ice are available at this gas station and convenience store.

■ Little Amana Winery [10]

Telephone: 319-668-1011
Hours: Mon–Sat 9:00 am–8:00 pm, Sun 10:00 am–6:00 pm

Open since 1971, this winery offers fruit and table wine such as cranberry, plum, and rhubarb. An extensive gift shop is located on the ground level and features china, glassware, pottery, gift baskets and picnic baskets, smokers, trays, mugs and other beverage gift items, napkins, cards, and games. The winery is operated by the owners of Der Weinkeller winery in Amana.

■ Little Amana Woolen Outlet [8]

Telephone: 319-668-2841
Hours: daily 8:30 am–8:00 pm

The Woolen Outlet sells blankets produced at the Amana Woolen Mill in Amana. Shoppers can also purchase rugs, sweaters, moccasins, and many other items. Gift certificates are available.

■ Tanger Outlet Center [5]

Telephone: 319-668-2811/800-4-TANGER
Location: I-80 exit 220 North
Hours: Mon–Sat 9:00 am–9:00 pm, Sun 12:00 pm–6:00 pm

This popular factory outlet center offers over 65 brand name and designer stores including Bass, Brooks Brothers, Geoffrey Beene, Laura Ashley, Liz Clairborne, Mikasa, London Fog, Polo, Ralph Lauren, and Reebok. Several fast-food restaurants, including McDonalds, Arby's, and Pizza Hut, are in the mall area (no need to repark), and nearby are several lodging facilities.

Tourist Assistance Information

ATM Cash and Banking Machines

Automatic Teller Machines (ATMs) are located at the Amana Handimart/Nordy's Subs and Salads in Amana (open daily 6:00 am–11:00 pm., and until 1:00 am on Friday) and at the Firstar Bank (machine available 24 hours) located between Amana and Middle Amana near the intersection of highways 220 and 151.

Automobile Fuel and Services

Amana Handimart, Amana—319-622-3270, the only stop in the Colonies for fuel
Butch's, South Amana—319-622-3166 or 319-642-3245, repair and towing
Floyd's Auto and Truck Repair, South Amana—319-622-3524, repair and towing
Homestead Auto and Truck Wash, Homestead—located next to Colony Country Store

Laundromat

Amana has a coin-operated laundromat which is open daily from 6:00 am to 10:00 pm. Available are 10 washers, 10 dryers, a large-capacity washer, soap machine, soda machine, and counter tops for folding. It is located just west of the Smokehouse Square Antiques and the Amana Meat Shop and Smokehouse.

Law Enforcement

Emergency law enforcement—telephone 911
Iowa County Sheriff—319-642-3722
Iowa State Highway Patrol—800-525-5555

Medical Assistance

Emergency medical care—telephone 911
Amana Medical Clinic—319-622-3231, intersection of highways 151 and 220
Hospital—319-642-5543, Marengo, Iowa
Amana Pharmacy—319-622-3341, Amana Medical Clinic building, intersection of highways 151 and 220
Dentist—319-622-3150, Amana Medical Clinic building, intersection of highways 151 and 220

Post Offices and Zip Codes

Post offices are located in Amana, Homestead, Middle Amana, and South Amana. East Amana, High Amana, and West Amana are serviced by the Amana post office. You need not use a street address to correspond with a business or attraction in this guide. Simply write to them in the village and use the following zip codes: Amana-52203, East Amana-52203, High Amana-52203, Homestead-52236, Middle Amana-52307, South Amana-52334, West Amana 52203. The Little Amana interstate complex is serviced by the Williamsburg post office. The zip code is 52361.

Public and Handicap Restrooms

Public restrooms are available at Amana restaurants and at the Stone Hearth Bakery, the Amana Woolen Mill, the Amana Meat Shop and Smokehouse, the Amana General Store, and the

Amana Furniture Shop. Handicap accessible rest rooms are located at the restaurants, the Amana Furniture Shop, and the Amana Woolen Mill.

AREA RELIGIOUS SERVICES

■ AMANA CHURCH SOCIETY
Middle Amana Church—Sunday 8:30 am, German service, 10:30 am, English service; see Middle Amana Church listing in Middle Amana chapter for more information

■ BAPTIST
Victor Baptist—Victor, Sunday 9:30 am, 319-647-3466 or 647-3486

■ CATHOLIC
St. Patrick's—Marengo, Saturday 4:00 pm, Sunday 8:30 am, 319-642-5438
St. Mary's—Williamsburg, Saturday 5:30 pm, Sunday 10:00 am, 319-668-1397

■ LUTHERAN
First Lutheran (ELCA)—Conroy, Sunday 8:30 am, 319-662-4190 or 642-7274
Trinity Lutheran—Conroy, Sunday 9:30 am, 319-662-4108
St. John's Lutheran, rural Homestead, Sunday 10:00 am, 319-662-4286
St. John's Lutheran—Marengo, Sunday 7:30 am, 319-642-5452
St. Paul Lutheran—Williamsburg, Sunday 8:00 am, 319-662-4108
Immanuel Lutheran—rural Williamsburg, Sunday 9:00 am, 319-668-2372

■ METHODIST
United Methodist Church—Amana Convention and Visitors Center, Sunday 10:00 am, 319-622-6532

First United Methodist Church—Marengo, Sunday 10:00 am, 319-642-3146

St. Paul's United Methodist—Williamsburg, 11:00 am, 319-668-1963

Ohio United Methodist—rural Marengo, Sunday 9:00 am, 319-647-2266

■ PRESBYTERIAN

First Presbyterian—Williamsburg, Sunday 10:00 am, 319-668-1375

First Presbyterian—Marengo, Sunday 10:00 am, 319-642-5561

■ OTHER DENOMINATIONS

Church of the Nazarene—Marengo, Sunday 9:30 am, 319-642-3673

Fundamental Gospel Church—Marengo, Sunday 9:00 am or 2:00 pm, 319-623-3782

Kingdom Hall of Jehovah's Witnesses—Marengo, Sunday 9:30 am, 319-642-5687

Trinity United Church of Christ—Marengo, Sunday 9:00 am or 6:30 pm, 319-642-3887

Pleasant Grove Grace Brethren—North English, Sunday 9:30 am, 319-664-3568

West Union Mennonite—rural Parnell, Sunday 9:30 am, 319-646-6004

Further Reading

There are several books and publications concerning the Amana Colonies. Many of them are available in local shops, the Amana Colonies Visitors Center in Amana, and the Museum of Amana History in Amana.

The Museum of Amana History has an order form that lists a number of books and other publications regarding Amana. These include the publications listed below as well as a number of books on German culture and communal societies; English translations of inspired testimonies used by the Amana Church Society; and a series of pamphlets on the arts and crafts of the Colonies, including architecture, basket making, blacksmithing, calico prints, carpet weaving, craftwork for the kitchen and garden, hooked rugs, knitting, lithography, pottery, quilting, samplers and house blessings, tinsmithing, and utilitarian woodworking.

GENERAL HISTORY BOOKS, ARTS AND CRAFTS, AND PUBLICATIONS

The Amana Colonies: Seven Historic Villages, compiled by Joan Liffring-Zug, Amana Society, Amana, Iowa, 1993.

Amana: The Community of True Inspiration, by Bertha M. H. Shambaugh, State Historical Society of Iowa, 1908, reprinted by Penfield Press, Iowa City, Iowa, 1988.

Amana: From Pietist Sect to American Community, by Diane Barthel, University of Nebraska Press, Lincoln, Nebraska, 1984.

Amana That Was and Amana That Is, by Bertha M. H. Shambaugh, State Historical Society of Iowa, Iowa City, Iowa, 1932, reprinted by Arno Press, New York, 1976.

Amana Today: A History of the Amana Colonies from 1932 to the Present, by

Lawerence Rettig, Amana Society, Amana, Iowa, 1975.
The Amanas Yesterday: A Religious Communal Society, collected by Joan Liffring-Zug, Penfield Press, Iowa City, Iowa, 1975.
A Change and a Parting, by Barbara S. Yambura, Iowa State University Press, Ames, Iowa, 1960; 2nd edition, 1986.
Ghosts of the Amana Colonies, by Lori Erickson, Quixote Press, Sioux City, Iowa, 1988.
Historic Stories of the Amana Colonies, by Ted W. Heinze, privately published.
Hobelspaen, by Marie Selzer, Hobelspaen Publications, Amana, Iowa, 1985.
How It Was in the Communal Kitchens, by Jonathon Andelson and Marie Trumpold, privately published by R. Trumpold, Fairfield, Iowa, 1976.
Inspirations-Historie, three volumes, by Gottlieb Scheuner, translated by Janet W. Zuber, Amana Church Society, Amana, Iowa, 1977, 1978, 1987.
Kolonie-Deutsch: Life and Language in Amana, by Philip E. Webber, Iowa State University Press, Ames, Iowa, 1993.
Now Pitching: Bill Zuber from Amana, by Clifford Trumpold, Lakeside Press, Middle Amana, Iowa, 1992.
Remaining Faithful: Amana Folk Art in Transition, by Steve Ohrn, Iowa Department of Cultural Affairs, Des Moines, Iowa, 1988.
Seasons of Plenty, by Emilie Hoppe, Iowa State University Press, Ames, Iowa, 1994.
Seasons to Remember: Recollections of an Amana Childhood, by Henrietta M. Rugg, privately published, Middle Amana, Iowa, 1996.
The Story of an Amana Winemaker, by George Kraus and Mae Fritz, Penfield Press, Iowa City, Iowa, 1984.
Village Voices: Stories from the Amana Colonies, edited by Robert Wolf, Free River Press, Lansing, Iowa, 1996.
Willow Basketry of the Amana Colonies, by Joanna E. Schanz, Penfield Press, Iowa City, Iowa, 1986.

AMANA AND GERMAN COOKBOOKS

Amana Colony Recipes, Homestead Welfare Club, Homestead, Iowa, 1948, 1976.
Christmas Cookie Walk Collection, Amana Church Society, Amana, Iowa, 1995.

Further Reading

Cuisines of Germany, by Horst Schargenberg, Poseidon Press, New York, 1980.

German-American Life Recipes and Traditions, edited by John Zug and Karin Gottier, Penfield Press, Iowa City, Iowa, 1991.

German Cookery, by Elizabeth Schuler, Crown Publishers, Inc., New York, 1955, 1983.

German Recipes: Old World Specialties and Photography from the Amana Colonies, edited by Sue Toemig Goree and Joanne Asala, Penfield Press, Iowa City, Iowa, 1985.

Guten Appetit from Amana Kitchens: The Amana Heritage Society Cookbook, Amana Heritage Society, Amana, Iowa, 1985.

Honey Recipes from Amana, Amana Society, Amana, Iowa, 1978.

The New German Cookbook, by Jean Anderson and Hedy Wurz, Harper Collins, New York, 1993.

Oma's (Grandma's) Family Secrets: Generations of Amana Cooking, by Linda Selzer, privately published, Homestead, Iowa, 1996.

The Ronneburg Recipe Album, by Elsie Oehler, Ronneburg Restaurant, Amana, Iowa, 1981.

Seasons of Plenty, by Emilie Hoppe, Iowa State University Press, Ames, Iowa, 1994.

Subject Index

■ **Restaurants**

Amana Barn Restaurant—Amana, 33
Brick Haus Restaurant—Amana, 36
Colony Haus Restaurant—Little Amana, 160
Colony Inn Restaurant—Amana, 40
Colony Village Restaurant—Little Amana, 162
Homestead Kitchen—Homestead, 97
Ox Yoke Inn—Amana, 43
Pizza Factory and Grill—Middle Amana, 115
Player's Grill/Amana Colonies Golf Course—
  Middle Amana, 117
Ronneburg Restaurant—Amana, 46
Seven Villages Restaurant—Little Amana, 164
Bill Zuber's Dugout Restaurant—Homestead, 100

■ **Lodging in the Seven Villages**

Amana Colonies Golf Course Condominiums—
  Middle Amana, 119
Amana Colonies RV Park—Amana, 50
Bábi's Bed and Breakfast—South Amana, 137
Baeckerei Bed and Breakfast—South Amana, 139
Corner House Bed and Breakfast—West Amana, 150
Die Heimat Country Inn—Homestead, 103
Dusk to Dawn Bed and Breakfast—Middle Amana, 121
Guest House Motel—Amana, 51
Noé House Inn—Amana, 53
Rawson's Bed and Breakfast—Homestead, 106
Rose's Place Bed and Breakfast—Middle Amana, 123

■ Lodging at or near Little Amana

Amana Holiday Inn—Little Amana, 166
Best Western Quiet House Suites—Little Amana, Exit 220, 169
Comfort Inn—Little Amana, 167
Crest Motel—see Little Amana, Exit 220, 170
Day's Inn—Little Amana, 167
Loy's Bed and Breakfast—Little Amana, Exit 216, 171
Lucille's Bett und Breakfast—Little Amana, 168
My Little Inn—Little Amana, 168
Ramada Limited—Little Amana, Exit 220, 170
Super 8—Little Amana, Exit 225, 169
Super 8—Little Amana, Exit 220, 171

■ Specialty Food Stores

Amana Meat Shop and Smokehouse—Amana, 60
Amana Meat Shop and Smokehouse—Homestead, 110
Amana Stone Hearth Bakery—Amana, 61
Colony Cone—Amana, 66
Colony Inn Candy Store—Amana, 66
Fern Hill Gifts and Quilts—South Amana, 143
Hahn's Hearth Oven Bakery—Middle Amana, 130
Homestead Cider Mill—Homestead, 112
Nordy's Subs & Salads—Amana 76
The Pepper Mill—Homestead, 112
The Village Mall—Amana, 84
Village Pastry Shop—Amana, 76

■ Wineries/Microbrewery

Ackerman Winery and Cheese Shop—South Amana, 142
Der Weinkeller—Amana, 68
Ehrle Brothers Winery—Homestead, 111
Grape Vine Winery and Gift Shop—Amana, 70
Heritage Wine and Cheese Haus—Amana, 71

Little Amana Winery—Little Amana, 174
Millstream Brewing Company—Amana, 73
Old Wine Cellar Winery—Amana, 78
Sandstone Winery—Amana, 81
Village Winery and Gift Gallery—Amana, 85

■ Shops

Alma's Washhouse—Homestead, 109
Amana General Store—Amana, 58
Amana Woolen Mill—Amana, 62
Antiques and Things—Amana, 63
Antique Tower Haus—Amana, 63
Carol's Giftshop—Amana, 64
The Christmas Room—Amana, 64
Clothes Encounter—Amana, 65
Colony Country Store—Homestead, 111
Colony Gardens—Amana, 66
Colony Inn Candy Store—Amana, 66
Fern Hill Gifts and Quilts—South Amana, 143
Gingerbread House—Amana, 70
Great Midwest Leather—Amana, 70
Kitchen Sink—Amana, 72
Lehm Books and Gifts—Amana, 72
Little Amana General Store—Little Amana, 173
Little Amana Woolen Outlet—Little Amana, 174
Maddie's/Der Laden—Amana, 73
Olde World Lace Shoppe—Amana, 78
Old Fashioned High Amana General Store—High Amana, 94
The Pepper Mill—Homestead, 112
Red Fox Paper Den—Amana, 79
Red Geranium—Amana, 80
Santa's Sleigh—Amana, 81
Schnitzelbank—Amana, 82
Tiny Tim's Colony Christmas—Amana, 83
The Village Mall—Amana, 84
Village Leather Haus—Amana, 83

■ Christmas Shops

The Christmas Room—Amana, 64
Colony Gardens—Amana, 66
Country Connection—Amana, 67
Creative Colony—Amana, 68
Grape Vine Winery and Gift Shop—Amana, 70
Oma's Haus—Amana, 78
Santa's Sleigh—Amana, 81
Tiny Tim's Colony Christmas—Amana, 83
Village Winery and Gift Gallery—Amana, 85

■ Antiques

Antiques and Things—Amana, 63
Carole's Giftshop—Amana, 64
Cricket on the Hearth Antiques—West Amana, 154
Erenberger Antiques—Amana, 69
Fern Hill Gifts and Quilts—South Amana, 143
Granary Emporium—South Amana, 145
Renate's Antique Gallery—Amana, 80
Smokehouse Square Antiques—Amana, 82
Tick Tock Antiques—Amana, 82
West Amana General Store—West Amana, 155

■ Arts, Crafts and Furniture

Amana Arts Guild Center—High Amana, 93
Amana Farmer's Market—Amana, 57
Amana Furniture Shop—Amana, 57
Berger's Hand Woven Rugs—South Amana, 143
Broom and Basket Shop—Amana, 64
Broom and Basket Shop—West Amana, 153
Colony Candleworks—Amana, 65
Colony Dolls—Middle Amana, 128
Country Connection—Amana, 67

Creative Colony—Amana, 68
Fenn Works—Amana, 69
Flora 'n Fauna: Etc.—Little Amana, 172
Heritage Designs Needlework and Quilting—Amana, 71
Krauss Furniture and Clock Factory—South Amana, 145
Oak Ridge Gallery—Amana, 77
Old Creamery Theatre Company—Amana, 77
Oma's Haus—Amana, 78
Powder House—Amana, 79
Roger's Anvil/Industrial Machine Shop Museum—Amana, 80
Schanz Furniture and Refinishing Shop—South Amana, 146
Schanz Furniture and Gift Shop—West Amana, 155

■ Museums

Amana Community Church Museum—Homestead, 109
Communal Agriculture Museum—South Amana, 145
Communal Kitchen and Coopershop Museum—
    Middle Amana, 128
Industrial Machine Shop Museum/Roger's Anvil—Amana, 80
Museum of Amana History—Amana, 75
South Amana Barn Museum—South Amana, 146

■ Miscellaneous

Amana Colonies Golf Course—Middle Amana, 126
Amana Colonies Nature Trail—Homestead, 110
Amana Community Library—Middle Amana, 126
Amana Community Park—Middle Amana, 127
Amana Community Pool—Middle Amana, 127
Amana Heritage Society, 60
Amana Refrigeration—Middle Amana, 127
Cemeteries, 89
Lakeview Village Retirement Community—Middle Amana, 132
Lily Lake—Amana, 72
Tanger Outlet Center (shopping mall), 174

■ Travel Services

Amana Colonies Convention and Visitors Bureau—Amana, 56
Amana Colonies Visitors Center—Amana, 57
Amana Handimart—Amana, 59
ATM locations, 175
Automobile fuel and services, 175
Church services, 177
Colony Visits/Heritage Destinations—Amana, 67
Dentist—Amana, 176
Emergency medical care, 176
Fetzer's Standard—Little Amana, 172
Handicap accessible restrooms, 176
Hospital—Marengo, 176
Iowa Welcome Center—Little Amana, 173
Laundromat—Amana, 175
Law enforcement, 176
Little Amana HandiMart—Little Amana, 173
Medical assistance, 176
Pharmacy—Amana, 176
Post offices, 176
Public Restrooms, 176
Religious services, 177
Restrooms, 176
Village Tours and Guide Service—Amana, 85
Zip codes, 176

Index

A

Ackerman Winery and Cheese Shop—South Amana, 142
Alma's Washhouse—Homestead, 109
Amana Arts Guild Center—High Amana, 93
Amana Barn Restaurant—Amana, 33
Amana Church Society, 56
Amana Colonies Convention and Visitors Bureau—Amana, 56
Amana Colonies Golf Course—Middle Amana, 126
Amana Colonies Golf Course Condominiums—Middle Amana, 119
Amana Colonies Nature Trail—Homestead, 110
Amana Colonies RV Park—Amana, 50
Amana Colonies Visitors Center—Amana, 57
Amana Community Church Museum—Homestead, 109
Amana Community Library—Middle Amana, 126
Amana Community Park—Middle Amana, 127
Amana Community Pool—Middle Amana, 127
Amana Farmer's Market—Amana, 57
Amana Furniture Shop—Amana, 57
Amana General Store—Amana, 58
Amana Handimart—Amana, 59
Amana Heritage Society, 60
Amana history, 9
Amana Holiday Inn—Little Amana, 166
Amana Meat Shop and Smokehouse—Amana, 60
Amana Meat Shop and Smokehouse—Homestead, 110
Amana Refrigeration—Middle Amana, 127
Amana Stone Hearth Bakery—Amana, 61
Amana Woolen Mill—Amana, 62
Antique Tower Haus—Amana, 63
Antiques and Things—Amana, 63
ATM locations, 175
automobile fuel and services, 175

B

Bábi's Bed and Breakfast—South Amana, 137

Baeckerei Bed and Breakfast—South Amana, 139
Berger's Hand Woven Rugs—South Amana, 143
Best Western Quiet House Suites—Little Amana, Exit 220, 169
Brick Haus Restaurant—Amana, 36
Broom and Basket Shop—Amana, 64
Broom and Basket Shop—West Amana, 153

C

Carol's Giftshop—Amana, 64
cemeteries—East Amana, 89
Christmas Room—Amana, 64
church services, 177
Clothes Encounter—Amana, 65
Colony Candleworks—Amana, 65
Colony Cone—Amana, 66
Colony Country Store—Homestead, 111
Colony Dolls—Middle Amana, 128
Colony Gardens—Amana, 66
Colony Haus Restaurant—Little Amana, 160
Colony Inn Candy Store—Amana, 66
Colony Inn Restaurant—Amana, 40
Colony Village Restaurant—Little Amana, 162
Colony Visits/Heritage Destinations—Amana, 67
Comfort Inn—Little Amana, 167
Communal Agriculture Museum—South Amana, 143
Communal Kitchen and Coopershop Museum—Middle Amana, 128
Corner House Bed and Breakfast—West Amana, 150
Country Connection—Amana, 67
Creative Colony—Amana, 68
Crest Motel—Little Amana, Exit 220, 170
Cricket on the Hearth Antiques—West Amana, 154

D

Day's Inn—Little Amana, 167
dentist, 176
Der Weinkeller—Amana, 68
Die Heimat Country Inn—Homestead, 103
Dusk to Dawn Bed and Breakfast—Middle Amana, 121

E–F

Ehrle Brothers Winery—Homestead, 111
emergency medical assistance, 176
Erenberger Antiques—Amana, 69
Fenn Works—Amana, 69
Fern Hill Gifts and Quilts—South Amana, 143
Fetzer's Standard—Little Amana, 172
Flora 'n Fauna: Etc.—Little Amana, 172

G

Gingerbread House—Amana, 70
Granary Emporium—South Amana, 145
Grape Vine Winery and Gift Shop—Amana, 70
Great Midwest Leather—Amana, 70
Guest House Motel—Amana, 51

H–J

Hahn's Hearth Oven Bakery—Middle Amana, 130
handicap accessible restrooms, 176
Heritage Designs Needlework and Quilting—Amana, 71
Heritage Wine and Cheese Haus—Amana, 71
history of the Amana Colonies, 9
Homestead Cider Mill—Homestead, 112
Homestead Kitchen—Homestead, 97
hospital, 176
Iowa Welcome Center—Little Amana, 173

K–L

Kitchen Sink—Amana, 72
Krauss Furniture and Clock Factory—South Amana, 145
Lakeview Village Retirement Community—Middle Amana, 132
laundromat, 175
law enforcement, 176
Lehm Books and Gifts—Amana, 72
Lily Lake—Amana, 72
Little Amana General Store—Little Amana, 173
Little Amana HandiMart—Little Amana, 173
Little Amana Winery—Little Amana, 174
Little Amana Woolen Outlet—Little Amana, 174
Loy's Bed and Breakfast—Little Amana, Exit 216, 171
Lucille's Bett und Breakfast—Little Amana, 168

M–N

Maddie's/Der Laden—Amana, 73
medical assistance, 176
Middle Amana Church—Middle Amana, 132
millrace, 12
Millstream Brewing Company—Amana, 73
Museum of Amana History—Amana, 75
My Little Inn—Little Amana, 168
Noé House Inn—Amana, 53
Nordy's Subs & Salads—Amana, 76

O

Oak Ridge Gallery—Amana, 77
Old Creamery Theatre Company—Amana, 77

Old Fashioned High Amana General Store—High Amana, 94
Old Wine Cellar Winery—Amana, 78
Olde World Lace Shoppe—Amana, 78
Oma's Haus—Amana, 78
Ox Yoke Inn—Amana, 43

P–Q

The Pepper Mill—Homestead, 112
pharmacy, 176
Pizza Factory and Grill—Middle Amana, 115
Player's Grill/Amana Colonies Golf Course—Middle Amana, 117
post offices, 176
Powder House—Amana, 79
public restrooms, 176

R

Ramada Limited—Little Amana, Exit 220, 170
Rawson's Bed and Breakfast—Homestead, 106
Red Fox Paper Den—Amana, 79
Red Geranium—Amana, 80
Renate's Antique Gallery—Amana, 80
restrooms, 176
Roger's Anvil/Industrial Machine Shop Museum—Amana, 80
Ronneburg Restaurant—Amana, 46
Rose's Place Bed and Breakfast—Middle Amana, 123

S

Sandstone Winery—Amana, 81
Santa's Sleigh—Amana, 81
Schanz Furniture and Refinishing Shop—South Amana, 146
Schauz Furniture and Gift Shop—West Amana, 155
Schnitzelbank—Amana, 82
Seven Villages Restaurant—Little Amana, 164
Smokehouse Square Antiques—Amana, 82
South Amana Barn Museum—South Amana, 146
Super 8—Little Amana, Exit 225, 169
Super 8—Little Amana, Exit 220, 171

T

Tanger Outlet Center (shopping mall), 174
Tick Tock Antiques—Amana, 82
Tiny Tim's Colony Christmas—Amana, 83

V–Z

Village Leather Haus—Amana, 83
The Village Mall—Amana, 84
Village Pastry Shop—Amana, 84
Village Tours and Guide Service—Amana, 85
Village Winery and Gift

Gallery—Amana, 85
walking tours—see Amana Heritage Society, Amana, 60
West Amana General Store—West Amana, 155
Bill Zuber's Dugout Restaurant—Homestead, 100